To Bo . . .
and to Ib

How to Zig in a Zagging World

Unleashing Your Hidden Creativity

John M. Keil

Illustrations by
Rodney MacNicholl

John Wiley & Sons

New York • Chichester • Brisbane • Toronto • Singapore

Library of Congress Cataloging in Publication Data:

Keil, John M.
  How to zig in a zagging world.

  Bibliography: p.
  1. Creative ability in business.   I. Title.

HD53.K44   1987   650.1   87-25316

ISBN 0-471-63524-3
ISBN 0-471-85720-3 (pbk)

Printed in the United States of America

10 9 8 7 6 5 4 3 2 1

acknowledgments

In putting together these short sections (or "creative power bursts," as they once were going to be called before cooler heads prevailed) I've used material from my own experiences, from the writings and verbalizing of others, and from the philosophies of Dancer Fitzgerald Sample (now Saatchi & Saatchi DFS Compton), the advertising agency. I've tried to give credit where it's due. The opinions and theories are mine unless otherwise noted and do not reflect, to the best of my knowledge, the policies of any agency, company, or organization.

A number of people have been most helpful with suggestions and advice but perhaps the most influential has been John Mahaney, my easy-going editor who seems to give the right nudge at the appropriate time (that being when the author is in a receptive mood) and has been able to push and cajole this thing along and make the author—writer association a lot of fun.

Conversations with Suzanne Eichhorn, Tim Foote, Pat and Lloyd Hamilton, Don Jackson, Chauncey Karten, Joe Kastner, my children Peter, Nick, and Betsy, Floyd Miller, Andy Nathan, Len Schwartz, and others that I wish I could think of right now, have given me ideas and points of view that have been included.

Working with thoughtful people in the advertising agency business— Stan Becker, Arnold Brown, Cliff Fitzgerald, Marty Friedman, Fran Kennedy, Joe Mack, Pete McSpadden, Pat Peduto, George Shaver, Gary Susnjara, Stu Upson, Bill Vickery—have given me insights, experiences (good and bad) that have been included herein. Mary Grace, friend and copy editor, has done much more than check grammar, punctuation, and spelling. She's been a master (or mistress) of gently letting me know when something doesn't make sense. Barbara Ziegler, administrative assistant, has faithfully checked facts and figures, worked this thing through her word procesor, and stood by to unscramble me when my word processor has done something ill advised.

And as always, my wife Barbara, who has seen too many weekends and vacations drift into my world of private creativity, has been my most encouraging cheerleader, proofreader, and patient but firm critic.

To them, one and all, I give thanks. Now read on—and see if it was worth it.

contents

Continued . . .

part three

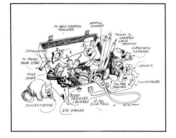

DR. KEIL'S TOOL KIT FOR ZIGGERS

part four

PUT IT DOWN: USING THE RIGHT SIDE TO GET IT ON PAPER

part five

UP AGAINST THE WALL

part six

SELLING IDEAS: THE ZIGGER'S WAY

Introduction: Zigging—More Important Than Ever

The world is made up of ziggers and zaggers and the theory is that there are more of the latter than the former.

Perhaps.

But not as many more as you might think. I believe that there is a lot of zigging ability in all of the so-called noncreative people. It's lurking, dozing, muttering, even trying occasionally to scratch its way out of the dark recesses of the cerebrum. And when it does surface we say, "Hey, I have an idea . . . " or "Listen, what if. . . ." We start to zig.

Unfortunately it seems to me that it's surfacing less than it did 20 or 30 years ago, or in World War II because crises, sadly, stimulate creativity. But there are other reasons why creativity is being squashed today:

Time

Anxiety

Pressure

'Tis wise to learn, 'tis God-like to create.
—John Godfrey Saxe, poet, *The Library*

We're living—no, existing—in an age where all three turn us into fast talking, almost gibbering boobs. The spoils are going to the quick and facile. Listen to these excerpts from a recent article in the *New York Times* special section on business. In his diary Peter G. Ziv was chronicling the events of his first two years as an investment banker.

"As the projects pile up, I find myself working longer and longer hours, arriving at the office by 8:30 A.M., leaving around 9 or 10 P.M."

". . . but it really angers her when I spend hours of a Cape Cod weekend crunching numbers on a portable computer."

"I leave the office at midnight Wednesday and I'm back by eight o'clock."

"By 2 A.M. I've finished three-quarters of the assignment."

"We are . . . driven, goal-oriented, and running on a fast track."

No great thing is created suddenly, any more than a bunch of grapes or a fig. If you tell me you desire a fig, I answer you that there must be time. Let it first blossom, then bear fruit, then ripen.
—Epictetus, *Discourses*

This may indeed be a fast, exciting, and momentarily rewarding track, but we're talking creativity here, which takes time for most of us. And time is what we don't have. We hear it all around us.

"I don't have time to think about where the company will be in the future. It's the next three months and the dividend that I'm worried about."

"We're having a meeting of the PTA steering committee Tuesday to recommend to the PTA executive committee Wednesday what they should bring up at the PTA board meeting on Thursday for discussion at the regular PTA meeting next Monday. No time for anything else."

"I hear it's a wonderful book—but I don't even have time to get through the *Daily News.*"

The pressures of a hi-tech computer age have robbed us of the time to do much more than react.

But there is hope.

This book (he said modestly).

Everyone can uncover some latent creative ability to help slip out of the time pressure cooker and make life richer, more rewarding, and more productive. This book tells you how.

The great law of culture is: Let each become all that he was created capable of being.
—Thomas Carlyle, *Essays*

These are fat words that promise a lot. But I think that anyone who has had anything to do with coming up with ideas knows that the fat words are true. I recently spoke at a conference on creation at the University of Rochester. A lot of impressive people were there. And one of the themes that kept coming through was the unbelievable high that the creative person has when a project is successfully completed. Rollo May, a founder of humanistic psychology, wrote: "Creativity . . . gives you the feeling that life is worthwhile," and "Our creativity is our divine spark; we become most like God at that point."

Another characteristic that swirled through the conference was the exuberance of all the speakers, no matter what their field: Sir Fred Hoyle, the legendary Cambridge professor of astronomy; Harlan Ellison, the prolific and widely read writer; Judy Chicago, the feminist artist; William Masters, the sex expert; Rutan and Yeager, who had just flown around the world on a tank of gas. They all bubbled over when talking about their work and their lives. Creativity keeps you that way.

It can also open whole new areas for you. It's like exploring a different country. Gets you out of a rut. Opens new vistas. It's a new day, especially if you're using creativity on other than your regular routine. You can become multifaceted. We saw this at the Rochester conference. These big-time creators had so much right-brain energy that it would spill over and come out in different areas. The paleontologist who came to talk and to sing Haydn's "Creation." The writer who used one-liners with the aplomb of a Catskill resort tummler. Even the president of the university, Dennis O'Brien, a philosopher, lecturer, mimic, teacher, administrator, wood sculptor, writer, and superb storyteller, carried out—or perhaps set—the tone. Actually, the title of his latest book, *God and the New Haven Railway and Why Neither One Is Doing Very Well*, may be a prime example of the zigger's mind at work.

Finally, I think that the art of putting this latent creativity to work can create habits, energy, a glow that carries over into other tasks and makes them come alive. An interesting experiment in the East Harlem School of Performing Arts in New York City seems to lend some credence to this theory. They've found that teenagers who bounce through an ultrastimulating dance or art class are bringing new energies and approaches to, say, biology or American history. There's a kind of spreading effect.

Before getting on with it, we should spend a few words refreshing you on the left-brain—right-brain theory. While there still seems to be some discussion and investigation of this, I am using it throughout the book because, to me, it

If a man has a talent and cannot use it, he has failed. If he has a talent and uses only half of it, he has partly failed. If he has a talent and learns somehow to use the whole of it, he has gloriously succeeded, and won a satisfaction and a triumph few men ever know.
—Thomas Wolfe, *The Web and the Rock*

explains a lot about what's happening upstairs. As you've read, the left brain purportedly controls the linear, logical, no nonsense, right-down-the-middle functions. It's also the voluble part of the brain. The right side is the dreamer, the imaginative, undisciplined, idea side. I like to think of them as Laurel and Hardy with Ollie the left side and Stan, the believer in black magic, the right.

> **OLLIE:** Well, Stanley, how on earth are we going to get in the house at this late hour without our wives finding out?
>
> **STAN:** That's easy, Ollie. We'll tell them we've been to a masquerade party.
>
> **OLLIE:** What in the world are you talking about?
>
> **STAN:** We'll tell them it's a masquerade and we're not really us.
>
> **OLLIE:** (long pause) Say that again.
>
> **STAN:** We'll tell them that us is not we. We're somebody else and then they won't be able to get mad at us.
>
> **OLLIE:** That's a good idea, Stanley, you've done it again.

What this book is about is developing the Stanley in all of us. It's not scholarly. It's not theoretical. It is practical. And I hope it's useful. The opinions are mine unless otherwise noted. They came from my own experience or the experiences of authors I've read or people with whom I've talked, but they are not a compendium of the aggregate thoughts of others.

part one

WHO, ME? ZIG?

chapter 1

DON'T WORRY, YOU'VE GOT IT, AND YOU CAN DO IT

If it's the ability to be imaginative, innovative, creative, you've got it. As I said, it may be lurking somewhere in the right side of your brain waiting to be prodded, stimulated, or awakened.

But it's there.

To a greater or lesser degree.

If it's greater, you know it. It bubbles out in the way you arrange flowers or write a letter home or doodle. If it's less, you may be the kind of person who wanders around saying, "Oh, I can't do that. My mind just doesn't work that way. I'm not the creative type." The reason that these people aren't the creative type is that they don't think they are. And so they aren't. They go by the book. But if they forced themselves to look at things differently, they might open the door on the right side a crack and watch a glimmer of creativity slip out.

Or they may be the kind who constantly say, "I've got a lot of creative things I want to do—and I'm going to do them, believe me, I am, as soon as I get a little time." These are people who don't have enough right-side chutzpah. The left side is cleverly plugging the creative fountain by steadily keeping the schedule jammed with real or perceived tasks. And when there is time for the right side to work, left side nudges it into somnolence by convincing it that "what we need now is a little rest and relaxation. Then, when we're refreshed, you can take off on your creative

> The artist produces for the liberation of his soul. It is his nature to create as it is the nature of water to run down hill.
> —W. Somerset Maugham, *The Summing Up*

> The world will never starve for wonders; but only for want of wonder.
> —Gilbert Keith Chesterton, inscription on G. M. Building, Century of Progress, Chicago, 1932

> Making a book is a craft, as is making a clock; it takes more than wit to be an author.
> —De la Bruyère, *Characters*

projects." Of course, left side makes sure that that time never comes.

To see where you stand in the world of creativity, take a survey. All strong creative people seem to possess five characteristics, which are described in the following five sections.

After reading each of these, step back and survey yourself as objectively as possible. On a scale of one to five (with five highest) rank yourself in each category. If you total 15 or more you probably have strong creative tendencies. But if you're below that, this book could help you improve the weak areas—and build on the strong ones.

chapter 2

BEFORE GOING WITH THE FLOW, ZIG

Creative people are independent. They learn to consider zigging when everyone else is zagging. This is another way of looking at things differently. Of course, when you do this, be prepared for some grumping and carping from others because you're going against the grain, as we used to say about him who wanders the wrong way in a wheat field. And the reason people don't like your approach is usually that it's different. "That's not the way it's done," they mutter. Or, "It makes me uncomfortable."

For a long time, in the world of television commercials there were some acceptable rules for casting. People had to be idealized. The audience did not want to see them as they really are but rather as they thought they should be. There were no crooked noses or moles or receding chins or fat people in TV land. Children were blond or red-haired and freckled with a tooth missing and a baseball cap worn askew. Smart kids wore horn-rimmed glasses. Then someone zigged.

His name is Joe Sedelmaier. He's famous for creating a whole new school, a whole new approach to selling products on TV. He used real people. An ex-manicurist became famous as the little old lady looking for the beef. A portly gentleman with a bewildered look stared at a TV set gone berserk in a bank. Sedelmaier's world was full of the fat, the old, the thin, big noses, bushy eyebrows, henna rinses—all blended together with warmth and humor. But in the beginning some critics disagreed. "Builds a negative atmos-

In matters of thought and conduct, to be independent is to be abnormal, to be abnormal is to be detested.
    —Ambrose Bierce, *The Devil's Dictionary*

phere," they said. "They'll turn the public off," they said. "Ruin our image," they said.

If you're exposed to television at all, you know that these commercials did and do turn the public on. An exciting new way of getting the public's attention came into being due, in large part, to the zigging of one man.

But if we, in our creative endeavors, bow to pressures from others, if we begin to care inordinately about each other's opinions, we'll begin to change things to please—and originality will slip out the door. Talented creative people try to maintain independent thought processes. One of the best ways to develop this independence is to solve a problem with the obvious approach—even if the obvious way seems to be the correct way. Then do the same thing again—only this time using a different approach. This can accomplish two things. (1) It can open the door to a whole new direction, something so revolutionary that it rides over the top of what seemed to be obvious. (2) It can become an exercise in independent thinking, to get the mind in the habit of questioning, going beyond the usual, looking at things differently. Zigging.

An example. The problem: Convenience and safety at dawn, dusk, and night for the amazing number of joggers and road runners who don't like to give up their daily workouts when they travel. The problem, of course, is packing their paraphernalia—shoes, shorts, socks, and, if it's cool, sweat suits. Invariably they forget the reflector vests. The zagger's rational answer: A jogger's checklist that is kept in the traveling kit as a reminder. The zigger's answer: Have hotels provide everything but shoes for a slight fee. And have the sweats and running shirts emblazoned with hotel name and phone number in reflecting paint. This does three things: (1) makes travel easier and lighter for the jogger, (2) provides a built-in safety device as well as local address in case of emergency, and (3) gives a little free advertising to the hotel.

To me this is going beyond the obvious to top a seemingly good idea. Notice that in doing this we played off of a

Let me exhort everyone to do their utmost to think outside and beyond our present circle of ideas.
—Richard Jeffries, *The Story of My Heart*

The indefatigable pursuit of an unattainable perfection, even though it consist in nothing more than the pounding of an old piano, alone gives a meaning to our life . . .
—Logan Pearsall Smith, *Afterthoughts*

weakness in the original concept—having to carry more than you want. This is really where the zigging thought process begins. But if there are no holes in the basic idea fabric, keep zigging anyway. You may come up with something new that cannot be denied.

As you'll see (and may have gleaned from the title) this is a basic theme of this book. I've treated it rather cavalierly in this section. It's fine to say "think differently" but doing it may be something else. That's why I'll try to cover a variety of different ways to stimulate thinking in a zigging mode. But there is at least one caution. Thinking differently does not necessarily mean thinking right. Young, exuberant creative people often say, "It's not right unless it's different." And there are times when the obvious way, the zagging approach, may be the correct one. The creative challenge may then be to make the obvious seem different, fresh, rewarding. Good writers know this well. John McPhee is a master of presenting his subject, whether it's the schists of Wyoming or a family doctor in Maine, in a straightforward yet original and imaginative style.

Now grade yourself. Ask yourself if you really are independent. Or do you follow the flow, react to stimuli in an expected way? We all like to think of ourselves as great individualists—but most of us aren't. That doesn't mean that we can't learn to question, to think differently, to be ziggers to a certain degree, at least. But to find out what your starting point is in the creative spectrum, pencil in your appraisal in the box.

> **Conformity is the jailer of freedom and the enemy of growth.**
> —John F. Kennedy, United Nations

> **Don't raise the bridge, just lower the river.**
> —George Brunis, during break in trombone solo of "I Wish I Could Shimmy Like My Sister Kate."

On a basis of one to five (five highest), my rating on independent thinking is _____ .

chapter 3

THINK LIKE A CHILD

The second of the qualities that most creative people have is that they're curious. As children, we all were. But somewhere along the way, that wondering-questioning-how-come-and-why world begins to dwindle as we accept the rules and guidelines that are imposed on us as we grow up. Curiosity becomes less dominant the older we get. At least, for most of us. But not for everyone. People who have developed their creativity want to know who said what and why and what made them say it, and what their relations were to the person to whom they were speaking. They want to know why a 24-valve engine is better. Or how a photographer managed to get perfect back lighting on an obviously candid shot. Or why songs built on a dominant chord structure seem to be easier to remember. They ask why and how come quite a bit. It's one of the first steps to getting to the "what if" or zigging question.

One way to rekindle the inquisitive flame is to start thinking like a child again. We're not talking about walking around asking why the sky is blue or why Daddy doesn't have any hair but rather to be curious about things going on around you. Next time you're in a bus just staring out the window in a semicomatose state, waiting to go the 14 blocks to your stop, look at the people and wonder about them. Why is that attractive girl arguing with the boy with the presentation case? What does the old man have in the big package? It looks heavy—but it's not because he's swinging it as he walks. What's in it? Where is he going with it? Pretty soon you'll find your observations and curiosity leading you to stories about the people who flash by.

Curiosity is free-wheeling intelligence.
—**Alistair Cooke,** *Vogue*

He who asks questions cannot avoid the answers.
—**Cameroon proverb**

I know of a doctor who still practices the curiosity game that he played in medical school. He would sit on the subway or bus and try to diagnose the health problems of the people around him from their appearance and mannerisms. (Man is leaning to the left as he walks. Curvature of the spine is probably giving him a lower back problem. Woman next to him is slightly popeyed. Possible thyroid problem. Red nose two seats away is into the juice and suffering from hypertension.) Pretty soon you'll find yourself being curious about not just the people but about everything. In this way the curiosity game can bring back your inquisitiveness, heighten your powers of observation, and stimulate the tendency to look at things differently.

Again be honest with yourself in using the box to grade yourself on how curious you are.

On a basis of one to five (five highest) my rating on being curious is _____ .

---

chapter 4

STAY LOOSE

Flexibility—another characteristic of the right side. We often think that true creativity means no compromise. Probably true if we're in the same league as someone like Picasso. Unfortunately, most of us aren't. We have to listen to and react to what other people think. That's why it's important to keep any rigidity in the left side of the brain where it seems to fit more naturally. When it sneaks into the right side it causes problems—a bulldog, no-compromise no-change attitude that can waste time, stifle new ideas, new approaches, other ways to look at things.

The challenge is to know when to be flexible and when not to give an inch. It's easier to be rigid when you have only yourself to please. ("I don't care what anyone else thinks. I like what I've done and I don't want to change it.") Unfortunately most of us can't afford this luxury. We are not the ultimate judge of our work. An editor is. Or an art director. Or a reviewer. Or a client. Or a husband or wife. And almost always, friends, or even the public. The give-and-take that comes while working on a creative project or idea comes with experience. But in the beginning it's probably better to lean on the side of "take." Listen to the comments of others; they may save you extra work, anguish, and disappointment.

What you have to do is train yourself to assume that your critics know what they're talking about (most difficult when they are tearing apart your best efforts) and then act on their suggestions, even if you disagree with them. Do it. Then compare the results with your original work. One of two things will happen. Either you'll prove that they are

> If I bind my will I strangle creation.
> —George Bernard Shaw, *Back to Methuselah*

> A wise man changes his mind, a fool never will.
> —Spanish proverb

wrong and you're right or, heaven forbid, the opposite. If they're right, you'll know as you begin to develop the case. And by doing this you've begun an exercise in flexibility and objectivity. Of course, it can be annoying and frustrating and aggravating and time consuming to go through this process but it's worth it—especially when you come up with something better. And each time you do it you're becoming less rigid. You're finding out that there is more than one way to zig.

When McGruff, the crime dog, was conceived, he grew from a strategy based on the realization that it is impractical to think the public will believe that crime can be abolished. But it can be nibbled at. Thrown off balance. Made less dangerous in certain ways. And there are things people can do to achieve this. Thus the theme line, "Take a bite out of crime." And this now familiar phrase, arrived at while I waited for a plane to be repaired in the middle of the night at the Kansas City airport, naturally led to the use of a canine as our spokesperson. But what kind of dog? I sketched on a yellow-lined legal pad all of the way from Kansas to New York. All cop dogs. And I was proud of my work. They all came out looking like pseudo Snoopies in Keystone Cop attire. I was sold. I presented the concept and hero dog to my cohorts. They were delighted with the idea but dubious about my dog. Too cute, they said. Dog must be a father figure. Someone people will listen to and admire. Look at Smokey the Bear, they said. We know he knows what he's talking about. I was adamant. I was going through creative pride of ownership. Keystone Cop dog was right because it was mine. But knowing that I had a strong vote in the final say, I let the others send in their suggestions. Keep the troops happy. And they came in droves. All kinds of dogs. A marvelous golden retriever with paws folded across his chest called Sarge. A bulldog named J. Edgar Dog. A wimp dog that turned into "wonderdog" when he saw a crime committed. And still my Keystone Cop beagle type was my first choice.

And then in came an art director and copywriter with McGruff. Tired, wise, warm, understanding—a trench-coated version of all the private eyes we'd ever known. A dog that had been around and seen it all. A dog that was appealing and that everyone could relate to.

And he was not officially a cop.

Or a private detective.

But he did represent the wisdom and understanding that we needed on the side of law enforcement. And with that, all of the other candidates faded into the background, becoming a part of the creative process that led up to the final zig, the now famous McGruff.

Flexibility, the ability to bend and change course, to adapt, is perhaps more of a practical creative characteristic than an intrinsic one. Think of your attitude and response to various situations in the past when you grade yourself.

On a basis of one to five (five highest) my rating on being flexible is _____ .

---

chapter 5

BE A PROBLEM SOLVER

Willingness to solve problems, even relishing it, is a clue to those with creative leanings. One of my problems in writing this book is that it's colored by my own experiences, principally in the advertising agency business. If I'm going to be at all successful in showing you how to do some zigging by thinking creatively, I'll have to bring in examples from other fields of endeavor. How well I do this will reflect the creativity of my problem solving ability. And there are ways to develop problem-solving techniques, which we'll go into later.

Writers should enjoy the problem of plotting. Hopper certainly accepted and then solved the challenge of light and shadow. A stage director looks forward to the problems of staging, character development, interrelationships. A film director delights in answering the problem of pacing and flow. Solving a problem creatively is a part of the delight of any profession or avocation. Chauncey F. Korten, an ex-art director and professor of art emeritus at the University of Michigan, is a good example. In his current life he's consulting with a number of businesses, solving their marketing problems. (A right-sider who is deeply involved in the left side. Mixing an artist with the marketing process could be like casting Bette Midler as Joan of Arc. But Korten is doing it successfully.) He revels in problem solving of any kind. Among other things, he's currently building his own house on Block Island. He's designed a kind of atrium in the center in which a spiral staircase curls three floors up to a glass-enclosed watch tower looking out on Block Island Sound and the coast. Each of the floors opens on to the atrium.

Problems are only opportunities in work clothes.
—Henry J. Kaiser, industrialist

19

Problem: Sun beats down on the glass and keeps the tower almost unbearably hot in the summer. In the winter, heat from the other rooms rushes into the atrium and rises to the top, concentrating the heat in the tower where it's not really needed. Karten solution: A 10-inch pipe down the wall of the atrium with openings in each of the rooms and built-in vacuum motors that suck the heat from the top and distribute it downward and through the rest of the house. In the summer he opens windows in the tower and the constant Block Island breeze dissipates the heat. I suppose he could also reverse the fan process pulling cool air through the lower rooms and helping to push the hot air out the top. Anyway, it's a nifty solution with a monumental saving in fuel bills. All accomplished by a very handy ex-art director who wallows in the fun of problem solving.

Problem solving is basic to success in a lot of fields. But if it isn't your forte, that does not necessarily mean that you don't have creative ability. It's just that most intuitive right-siders are heavy in this area. Actually, it's the outstanding example of the left and right sides working together.

On a basis of one to five (five highest) my rating on enjoying problem solving is _____ .

chapter 6

EUREKA!

Whether or not being spontaneous is a trait that indicates strong creativity is probably debatable. There are certainly thoughtful, careful, measured thinkers who are extremely creative. But if they're not spontaneous they can miss the "eureka" experience. As an idea flashes across the right side, instead of saying, "Wow. That's it," and acting on it, their left side steps in and says, "Hmmm. Interesting. Let's look at all the pros and cons. I wonder if it's worth thinking about. I'll give it some consideration tomorrow—but mustn't be compulsive about this. Don't want to waste a lot of time on something that won't be fruitful." Be impulsive, snatch at the idea before it drifts away. Work on it. Develop it. You can always say, "Nah, it's not right" later. But, if you never act spontaneously, you may never have a chance to shout "Eureka!"

One Way to Get to Eureka

Can you train yourself to be more spontaneous? I think so. Practice the thought-association exercise. Goes something like this. Relax in a room with a group of people, usually not more than five or fewer than three. Pick a topic. One person makes a statement. Next person lets a word from the statement trigger a thought and develops something— another thought, a rhyme, a word play, a song title, something. Next participant does the same. And everything must be done fast so that there's no time for thinking. It can be senseless, hilarious, embarrassing, thought provoking, but

> In the matter of ideas he who meditates is lost.
> —William McFee, "The Idea," *Harbours of Memory*

> Eureka!
> —Archimedes (upon finding the principle of specific gravity)

> The whole difference between construction and creation is exactly this: that a thing constructed can only be loved after it is constructed; but a thing created is loved before it exists.
> —Gilbert Keith Chesterton, preface to Dickens' *Pickwick Papers*

it's a way to get into the rhythm of spontaneity. And it can get the right side in the habit of working impulsively once again, just as it used to do when you were a child, before the world of rules and guidelines and caution. We use this technique from time to time to solve advertising problems, putting the results on tape. Here's an example that could easily have happened.

NO. 1: Who likes Cocoa Puffs?

NO. 2: Who likes cuckoo puffs?

NO. 3: The cocoa bird likes cuckoo puffs.

NO. 4: The cocoa bird huffs and puffs.

NO. 1: . . . and blows the mouse down.

NO. 2: The mouse gives the bird the bird.

NO. 3: The mouse drives the cocoa bird cuckoo.

NO. 4: No. The cuckoo bird drives the mouse cocoa.

NO. 1: The mouse goes loco with cocoa.

And so forth.

Usually this kind of thing among creative professionals can produce ideas that can be quickly built into a campaign. I say quickly because professionals in the business are trained and experienced enough to translate the idea into a workable advertising format in a minimum of time. According to Roy Rowan in his book *The Intuitive Manager*, Edwin Land, founder of Polaroid, says, "There is no such thing as group originality, group creativity . . ." Maybe. But even if conclusions can't be drawn by consensus, these sessions can give stimulation that leads to individual answers. And if it doesn't come easily, if the exercise seemingly drifts in and out of non sequiturs with nothing building or happening, go back and listen to the tapes. Perhaps something has been missed, something that will be the key to an idea. In this example the words cuckoo and cocoa keep appearing. A cuckoo bird also makes an appearance. A cuckoo bird goes cuckoo. And of course the next step is that the cuckoo bird

The individual never asserts himself more than when he forgets himself.
—Andre Gide, *Portraits and Aphorisims*, Pretext

goes cuckoo for Cocoa Puffs. And there is the idea. An idea that became a campaign for this General Mills cereal that has been titillating children and making money for over 20 years. Actually, this kind of exercise in group spontaneity has been the source of a number of advertising campaign ideas.

Of course preparing for spontaneity is a discipline in itself. It calls for gathering information, studying, filling the pot that simmers somewhere on the back burner of the right side. Without that, there's nothing to fuel the train of thought, which is constantly subconsciously brewing all of the factors that can or may or will someday come together and bubble forth with what may seem to be a spontaneous answer, idea, solution, or random thought. Knowing your subject thoroughly is one of the best ways that I can think of to give yourself a chance to shout "Eureka!"

On a basis of one to five (five highest) my rating on being spontaneous is _____ .

Now total your scores for independence, curiosity, flexibility, problem solving, spontaneity. Twenty-five means that you can probably write this book. (I've made an okay living being creative and I check in at 22.) Around 20 and you should be working in some creative job; 15 to 20, consider strengthening the weak areas—it will be worth it. Below 15, your creative tendencies have been sublimated. But with awareness, concentration, and practice they can come forth.

part two

UNLEASHING IT

chapter 7

CREATIVE PEOPLE ARE GENIUSES, RIGHT? WRONG!!

Quite a few famous creative people have high I.Q.s. And quite a few don't. Intelligence is not necessarily a big part of the creative psyche. Fredelle Maynard, in her book *Guiding Your Child to a More Creative Life*, states that according to a test given by the University of Minnesota, 70% of the most creative elementary school children tested failed to look good on the standard intelligence tests. She goes on to say that "divergent thinking: exploratory, venturesome, free-wheeling characterize all creative activity. It has little to do with I.Q." Later she reminds us that one of Edison's teachers wrote his mother that he was "inattentive, indolent and his brain is severely addled."

All of this is fine, if you intend to follow a purely creative life with other people doing the planning, thinking, marketing, analyzing for you. But that's not most of us. If we intend to use our creativity to make a living—and our left side can't pick up the logical thinking that's needed to complete the circle—we'd better not try to do it alone. I've seen too many creative people who present an idea and then when asked how and why they arrived at it reply, "Beats the hell out of me, but isn't it wonderful?" It may be. But there's a good chance that it will go nowhere without someone to explain why it should exist or what need it will fulfill. And the more different the idea or concept, the more it needs to have some kind of explanation.

The sign of an intelligent people is their ability to control emotions by the application of reason.
—Marya Mannes, *More in Anger*

To put it another way, I think leaders in any field have to have a number of qualities—intelligence, intuition, creativity, empathy, vision, indefatigability, and charisma. Few have all of these but most have a majority. But to be true leaders there is one they must have, and it isn't creativity. It's intelligence. If they happen to be extremely creative but low on intelligence, they should never try to be a leader. They should be happy with the reward of creating. Thus, if you don't have to be smart to be creative, you should have access to some smarts to help you do with your creative results what you want done.

chapter 8

ON MAKING TIME FOR ZIGGING

It's fine to discipline yourself to allow time to be creative, if you can do that. But many of us can't. We plan to really sit down and paint or write or play the piano or compose. We look forward to it. Sometimes we use it as a reward to be savored when we finish the work of the day. But somehow we never quite get there because time evaporates, owing to many factors, some of which I mentioned in the introduction. But if you want to enjoy the fun of exercising the right side of the brain, you've got to make time.

This is where the left side can become a pseudo partner. Let it be the scheduler, monitor, and police officer of your time. Of course the problem here is we're assuming that both sides use the same logic and reasoning. It would be fine if things went like this:

> **LEFT SIDE:** OK, righty, here's the schedule I've worked out. We get the regular jobs done by noon. We cut down the dawdling at lunch. We do the shopping right after lunch and that gives you from three until five every day to be creative. Two whole hours . . . every day. Ten hours a week!
>
> **RIGHT SIDE:** You got it. From three to five every day I'm going to churn out stuff like you'd never believe.

But things don't go like that, because right side's natural lack of discipline and fear of regimentation enter the scene. And so instead . . .

> **A man may write at any time, if he will set himself doggedly to it.**
> —Samuel Johnson, quoted in Boswell's *Journal of a Tour of the Hebrides with Samuel Johnson*

RIGHT SIDE: Wait a minute. Back up the truck. What if I don't feel like it at three o'clock? What if some afternoon I can't do it? What if I'd rather do my creating first thing in the morning, or late at night. It's not a faucet, ya know. You don't just turn the creative juices on and off.

LEFT SIDE: (resigned sigh) Look, bunglehead. I really don't care when you do it, just so you do it. The important thing for you to realize is that I can make time in your busy schedule by doing a little preplanning.

RIGHT SIDE: But . . . but I just can't be sure I can create at the same time every day . . . (fades into whimpering).

LEFT SIDE: Okay, let's try it day by day. Each night we'll sit down and go over the next day's schedule and work out the time that you think will be best.

RIGHT SIDE: (taking another tack) But how are we gonna get two hours out of every day? I'm busy all the time.

LEFT SIDE: That's because you're not letting me organize you. If we just eliminated the time you waste. . . .

RIGHT SIDE: (indignant) I do not waste time.

LEFT SIDE: . . . doing the crossword puzzle and having that extra cup of coffee in the morning. The secret is getting what you have to do in 70% of the time it usually takes you.

RIGHT SIDE: You can do that?

LEFT SIDE: That's my job, kiddo. I'll make the time. You make the ideas.

In the business world where, as we touched on in the introduction, time is the culprit that's robbing our zigging abilities, I've felt that this type of planning could be put to productive use. Assiduously work at eliminating an hour and a half of procrastination and waste per day. Put those saved hours in the bank and spend them periodically. Every

10 days or so dedicate an entire day to creative stimulation. Think of the effect of coming into the office to lectures and symposiums and film festivals and brainstorming sessions and cross pollination of ideas with people you didn't even know existed.

It's a workable idea if it's carefully planned. It takes commitment and discipline. The time must be saved and banked and then used to excite the right side, not to do just more of the routine. It could make a lot of lives less ratty and racy. And it could open new vistas and visions and opportunities to a lot of organizations.

Now, back from the organization person to the individual. Obviously, saving time and using it wisely will be easier if you can find out if there's a special time when you seem to be at your zigging best. From three to five may be tired time, not relaxed time. I once knew a copywriter who was sensational early in the morning (or early in the moonin' as Jimmy Rushing used to say). He was in the office at seven and moving over the typewriter like a concert pianist. But by midafternoon he was through. Finished. Kaput. And so he went home. But he'd put in a full day's work. He'd found his optimum creative time and used it well.

The challenge is to find that time when you create best. With some it may be an emotional rhythm. I think the only way is to try different times, and when you hit the one that seems best, try to arrange the rest of your day around that time.

Sometimes uncontrollable events influence your zigging capabilities. They should be taken into account when you're trying to work out your creative periods. Some women not working outside the home (why am I nervous about using the term "housewife?") find that the flurry and turmoil of getting kids off to school and husband or partner off to work and straightening house and planning or doing shopping and the hundreds of other details that seem to go with keeping a household and family somewhat viable are not conducive to moving into the imaginative creative mode. They should probably plan their creative time for later, with

Asked why he did not go to the movies more often, T. S. Eliot replied, "Because they interfere with my daydreams."

some kind of decompression period first. And that decompression can be time for dreaming, for subconsciously preparing, for letting ideas drift in and out while you're reading the paper. But you should do it with the pad nearby so that you can jot down the words or random thoughts that may become creative prods. And it shouldn't be forced. The daydream is one of the most important stations for boarding the train of thought.

Another approach is to apply zigging to the entire daily routine. If these women find that they're inspired in the morning, that that's their creative time, then they should postpone the clean-up, straighten-up period. Who says the beds can't be made at four in the afternoon? On the other hand, housework, for some, can also be daydreaming time, preparation for the creative onslaught to come. The point is that if you have control of time arrange it to suit your needs and desires, not your habits.

Of course the problem for most of us is that we don't have that control. We have certain routines that have to be met, particularly if there's something as mundane as a job involved. Then the creative period usually has to be at night. Or before leaving for work. Or lunch hour. Or on the weekends. Think about those times and what you do now and how that can be adjusted. In emergencies we've all worked on projects—many of them creative—during crises. We've taken sandwiches up to our desk and worked through lunch. Or we've gotten up at six o'clock and finished the painting for the show before leaving for the office. Or we've put in an hour or so in the evening rather than trapping ourselves in front of the television set. Incidentally, if you do work in the evening and have certain sleep requirements, I've found that using the right side extensively just before going to bed does not make for blissfully slipping into dreamland. Either your eyes are staring at the ceiling with the unsolved problem still fresh in your mind or your legs are twitching with the adrenalin of accomplishment. Build in some wind-down time. Read the telephone book for a while. Or some such. My brother used to get copies of the Congressional Record, for some reason. I'd read those. That's a guaranteed paralyzer.

Each pro who has to create for a living works out a schedule that helps him produce his best. The aforementioned copywriter was an early morning person. The problem is that many of us are not working alone. We are dependent on others and the system. There are meetings to attend and briefings and deadlines and presentations. And most of these things happen at the behest of others. We have to make our schedules conform. We have to learn to put the right side into action any time, any place. But that is the subject for another tip, starting on the next page.

> A creative economy is the fuel of magnificence.
> —Ralph Waldo Emerson, *English Traits*

chapter 9

HOW TO PREPARE YOUR MOOD AND YOUR PLACE

Again we return to the example of free-flowing child creativity where the lack of restriction and boundaries lets the imagination soar. Children haven't learned what they can't do. In the very early years no one tries to inhibit them with rules. Unfortunately, this changes too soon through parent intervention. "Would you like to have fun with your clay, Nicky?" they say. Nicky's face lights up. "Okay then, sit down at your little table and let's put an apron on so that we don't get the stuff on our shorts, shall we?" Nicky's smile starts to fade. ". . . and keep the clay on this plastic doily so it doesn't get all over everything." Smile turns to frown. ". . . and don't make anything too high that might tip over and mess up the floor." Frown goes to pout. "Okay, go ahead and make what you want. Isn't this fun?"

"No."

"Honestly, I don't understand you. I thought you wanted to play with your clay."

Freedom is what Nicky wanted. Freedom to create without restrictions, real or emotional. Ed McCabe, one of advertising's most envied practitioners, in a speech before the National Radio Advertising Bureau Work Shop, quoted a nine-year-old Brandeis University study that reveals "freedom as the single best creative stimulant."

If so, then anything that you can do to ensure freedom before you start should help. Here are some things that I've found useful in establishing the freedom of a creative mood.

The misfortune which befalls man from his once having been a child is that his liberty was at first concealed from him, and all his life he will retain the nostalgia for a time when he was ignorant of its exigencies.
—Simone de Beauvoir, *Pour une morale de l'Ambiguïté*

1. If you have a choice, pick the right place. Interruptions and phone calls inhibit freedom and concentration. Try to have someone else handle them while you're working. Robert Massie, the author of *Nicholas and Alexandra*, even discontinued his local newspaper so that there would be no interruption for the weekly collection. (He had tried to pay a month in advance, but this didn't seem to be on the newspaper boy's agenda.) Some people like the completely bare room with no distractions. Others like familiar surroundings. As I write this I'm looking out over Block Island Sound on a July day. A marsh hawk is swooping below over the bayberry bushes. To me, it's not so much a distraction as a break. I find it restful and refreshing. I watch for a minute and then surge back to work. This is a matter of discipline, so find out what conditions relax you—even stimulate you—and then try to set up those conditions.

2. Now comes an interesting contradiction. Restrictions are often the key to greater freedom—they can act like a magnifying glass and bring focus and a resultant intensity to the right-side effort. Restrictions must not be walls that block but rather channels that guide the creative flow. One way is to plan some short-term goals. Set a time limit on what you want to accomplish. Don't say, "I'm going to sit right down and write Aunt Dot a long letter." Instead how about, "I have one hour before I have to do some errands so if I'm going to write Aunt Dot a letter I'd better jot down some things I want to say first so that I can get it done." Or, "I have three hours to work on the screenplay. I'll spend the time rewriting the third scene and not worry about anything else. But at the end I'll have it done."

3. Discipline yourself. This sounds like an outgrowth of short-term goals, but I mean it to be more. Sometimes we don't feel in the mood to create. We just don't want to. For the professional, these moods are dismissed as a natural thorn in the side of the profession. Whether you're an author, an advertising person, or a computer programmer, you have no choice. You have to produce. But the amateur, the person who's creating for her own pleasure, or for eventual public acclaim, can use any excuse she wants to keep from getting it done. The problem, of course, is that it doesn't get done. My way around this is to set a specific time aside for creativity and then ahead of that time think about what I'm going to do. As this goes on I find myself looking forward to the creative time. And when it comes, it's not hard to discipline myself to get to it.

4. Sometimes the working conditions have to be in the walls of your mind because often we have no control over our environment. In *The Creative Mystique* I talked about good creative professionals being able to do their job wherever they have to: on planes, or trains, during meetings, in crowded rooms or bullpens or beaches. I even know a copywriter who worked out a complete campaign at Yankee Stadium. (It was hard times for the home team that year.)

The tip here is to wall yourself in so that the mind becomes the arena where you practice creative freedom. Later, we'll talk about getting in the "right-side mode." It's a way to concentrate thoughts inward so that when you start, you're so involved that you become oblivious to your surroundings. Another way to accomplish this is to engage in some noncreative task in the alien environment, something that's demanding to the left side. Work with a pocket calculator on your expense account or balance your bank account or make a list of priorities coming up. Then slide into your creative task as your environment fades into the unimportant. You've used structure to warm you up and free your mind.

> **It is by losing himself . . . in inquiry, creation, and craft that a man becomes something.**
> —Paul Goodman, *The Community of Scholars*

chapter 10

THE ZIGGER'S
TIP SHEET

Here's a change of pace section that may give you some time and mind saving thoughts, many of them obvious but some that could be "Hey, that's a good idea" ideas. I've been talking about how to prepare your mind, your mood, and your place for optimum creative output. But you mustn't overlook some of the basic tools and left-side organizational details of getting the job done. And so herewith a list of suggestions to go over when you're ready to sit down and get started.

1. I use a spiral notebook rather than a legal pad for notes and rough stuff. With the legal pad I was always losing pages here and there. I try to transfer the material from the notebook into a first draft on the word processor as soon as possible to prevent the woe of lost notes.

2. I like to use pencils on the notebook, therefore I always carry a small pencil sharpener in my briefcase.

3. When I'm making or taking notes I use only three-quarters of the page, leaving a column down the right-hand side clear for sudden thoughts or ideas that I may want to use later. If I'm doing rough copy directly on the word processor and get a sudden extraneous thought, I skip a line, bang out three ***s, insert the thought, put in three more ***s to indicate end of thought, skip a line and go on with the original work. When I'm through, however, I try to remember to go back and check the ideas so that I don't end up three weeks later looking through the notebook and saying, "Oh, oh. I meant to include that earlier" or worse, "Huh. Wonder what I meant by that."

4. If I'm saving anything on floppy disks in the computer I don't use all the bytes. Once I wanted to add about five paragraphs to something I'd written earlier. Went back to the appropriate place in the disk and, of course, found that I'd filled same and there was no room for the new stuff to be inserted.

5. If possible, try to have a place to create where you can leave everything in midstream without having to put things away. Then you can start right in again next time without the problem of searching, trying to find your place, wondering what you did with the reference material, looking in the top drawer where you know you put the paint brushes. Makes it much easier to sit down and work when you have only limited time. And if you have lots of space, use it. Michelet, the French historian, felt that he was a better historian than most because he had a larger table.

6. If you're exploring the world of being an artist, always carry a small sketchbook and pens with you because sketching is a great way to keep the right side active, particularly when you're in one of those situations where you seem to be waiting . . . waiting . . . waiting. I have a gallery of quick sketches of people sitting in the air terminals of the world—Kennedy, Narita, Heathrow—waiting . . . waiting . . . waiting.

7. Write descriptions of the things going on around you, which is akin to keeping a daily journal. The beauty of the journal is that it not only helps you hone your writing skills, but it also builds your powers of observation, keeps your memory memorable as you reread what you've written years later, helps you practice selectivity and discernment. When you record the events of the day, you'll probably not do it chronologically but rather according to how those events strike you in importance. And, therefore, your faculties of discernment and judgment will get a daily work-

Imagination grows by exercise and contrary to common belief is more powerful in the mature than in the young.
—W. Somerset Maugham, *The Summing Up*

out. You might start by saying, "What is the one thing I want to remember about this day?"

8. When you write your journal, use only one side of the page. Then later on go back and reread it and use the back of the page for comments or additional thoughts or your own feelings about what happened then with the hindsight of perspective and experience. Often the journal can be the start and basis for something big. But allow the full page for these later thoughts. Gore Vidal once, when asked what he liked about being rich, replied that it allowed him the luxury of unlimited versions of his work because while as a writer he felt that he didn't have much to say, he always had lots to add. I'll cover what these versions might be later.

9. When you're writing your original rough copy use different underlining techniques. Straight line for important thoughts, wavy lines for quotes you may want to check later, dotted lines for facts and figures that have to be verified.

10. A friend of mine, Audrey Foote, seems to have a nice working relationship between her left and right sides, which makes her a supreme organizer of creative material. In doing research for an important paper on English literature, she used index cards of different colors for different subjects, which allowed her to shuffle the order any way she wanted before writing with the word processor.

11. Often we find ourselves working quite far in advance on creative projects. Or at least working from time to time quite far in advance. My topic at the "Creation" conference at the University of Rochester was "Creativity in a Hi-Tech Society." Although I had some ideas on the subject, I clipped everything I could find that might possibly relate to it and put the clippings in topic folders ("Creativity and Business," "Creativity as Therapy," "Creativity and Academia," and so forth). This helped me immeasurably in organizing the talk—and the material was both pertinent and up to date. The writer Jacques Barzun used to underline passages and have his secretary clip them and put them in various folders. At the end of six weeks or so he would lift each folder and the heaviest would be the subject for his next piece.

part three

DR. KEIL'S TOOL KIT FOR ZIGGERS

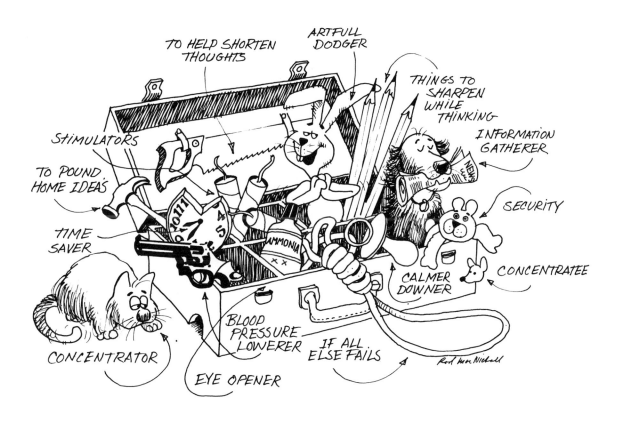

chapter 11

RIGHT-BRAIN STRATEGIES: FIVE QUESTIONS TO ASK YOURSELF

You can't get anywhere unless you know where you're going. In advertising we developed a device called the creative strategy that acts as a road map to show us where we're going and suggest how to get there. In explaining this in *The Creative Mystique* I made a remarkable discovery. The strategy is applicable to just about any creative task you might have or project you might be working on. It's been used to develop a point of view for the lyrics of a song, to write a proposal for a zoning change, to compose a grant application for a family resource center, to clarify thinking on a family problem.

Its strength is in its simplicity and logic. Its usefulness is directly proportional to its focus and specificity. And the reason I'm including it here is that not only is it an important part of the zigging process but it almost always acts as a stimulus to the right side. By the way, it's the classic example of logic and planning helping creativity.

Simply, to arrive at a strategy for zigging, you ask yourself five questions.

1. What are people's beliefs or perceptions, if any, of the project or idea or the circumstances surrounding it?

2. Whom are you trying to reach?

The mightiest rivers lose their force when split up into several streams.
—Ovid, *Love's Cure*

Give me the freedom of a tight strategy.
—Norman Berry, Creative President of Creative Worldwide, Ogilvy & Mather

3. What do you want them to do?

4. What is the key thought, the motivation that will make them do what you want them to do?

5. What is there about the key thought that will convince them that it's right?

Now a bit of explanation and clarification point by point. What are people's beliefs or perceptions?

This can be a most important influence on how your right side attacks the creative problem.

Example 1. If you're contemplating a letter home from college asking for money, think of the perceptions that your mother might have about you and college life. Not eating well. Staying up too late. Studying too hard. Living a life of debauchery. One of these could steer you into an approach that says, "Life is wonderful here—except for the food. I really am subsisting on Twinkies and potato chips because the dining hall food is atrocious—two-day old grey meat and congealed gravy. Unfortunately, I don't have enough money to go to the health food restaurant down the street or even for a decent meal at the student union. But everything else is fine, and so on."

Example 2. If you're opening a restaurant featuring a big rotisserie, what is the potential market's perception of France or a French sounding name? Okay in New York, San Francisco, or Los Angeles—but what about Duluth or El Paso? It might be just fine—one of the best French restaurants I've ever experienced is in Omaha—but you'd better find out. The perception can have a major influence on your creative positioning.

Example 3. You're a lawyer selecting a jury for an illegal arms dealer. Public perceptions: Arms dealers are bad because they make huge profits from an unpopular and sometimes shady occupation. There is no particular preperception about the individual client because he has operated in a low-key manner with no public image or pretrial publicity. He is in the courtroom. What will be the perceptions of him when the jurors first see him? He is a small, shy looking, unpretentious man. His name is Shapiro. The perceptions probably range from none to mild surprise. ("How could someone in this business look like that? Why, he looks like a teacher or the man in the Charmin commercials.") You note both of these perceptions—the negative attitude toward arms dealers and the fact that the defendant is Jewish.

In advertising we constantly search for these perceptions. Banks are cold and heartless. Used car salesmen are less than honest. Fast food is less than nutritious. Japanese cars are efficient and give great gas mileage. Compared to imports, U.S. cars have quality problems. True or not, perceptions exist, and in the advertising business if they're not reckoned with the results can be costly indeed.

Again, no matter what the creative challenge or project, look for perceptions. There may be none or they may not influence what you're going to do, but be aware of that, too.

> The fact that an opinion has been widely held is no evidence whatever that it is not entirely absurd; indeed in view of the silliness of the majority of mankind, a widespread belief is more likely to be foolish than sensible.
> —Bertrand Russell, "Christian Ethics," *Marriage and Morals*

Whom Are You Trying to Reach?

This may seem easy. The trick here is to be specific.

Example 1. Back to the restaurant. You're not gearing the place to everyone who eats out. Your price dictates upper middle class income, age group 30 to 50. Couples. These facts should be included in your audience description.

Example 2. The arms dealer trial. Whom do you want on that jury? Probably at least one Jewish mother. Specifically, who you're talking to can have a strong influence on your creative approach. And in this case your audience is not 12 people. Just one, the Jewish mother. Because all you have to do is convince one person and the required total of 12 votes goes out the window.

What Do You Want Your Audience to Do?

> A thought which does not result in an action is nothing much, and an action which does not proceed from a thought is nothing at all.
> —Georges Bernanos, "France Before the World of Tomorrow," *The Last Essays of Georges Bernanos*

Example 1. Do you want them to visit your restaurant? Seems obvious. But how about visit your restaurant rather than the three beefsteak houses down the street. Again, we're trying to be more specific and concentrate the creative focus. This might dictate a "change of pace" execution.

Example 2. In regard to the jury, you want them to find the client innocent of all charges. Or perhaps, according to your assessment of the case, find the client innocent of three of the four charges. Or even find him guilty of reduced charges. This section, in effect, becomes the "objective" of your creative efforts.

What Is the Key Thought?

Example 1. For the restaurant it may be that it brings an exciting new dining experience, outdoor grilling indoors, to the people of Toledo or Kansas City or Davenport.

Example 2. For the jurors it might be to have pity on this unfortunate man. ("Somewhere there is a mother, just like you, anguishing over the way her son has been manipulated by power brokers into this position.") Or if the evidence is overwhelming and you're working toward reduced charges it might be: "How could this man do anyone any harm? Look at him. Those eyes. That kind smile. Why, he could be your son." Anyway, you get the idea.

The important thing here is that we select one thing as the key thought, not a laundry list of ideas. People don't remember laundry lists. They water down the impact and diffuse the creative focus.

What Is There About the Thought That Makes It Believable?

This can be both simple and complex.

Example 1. The restaurant example becomes the proof or the reason why. The rotisserie. "We bring outdoor dining indoors because we have a new rotisserie."

No way of thinking or doing, however ancient, can be trusted without proof.
—Thoreau, "Economy," Walden

Example 2. The reason why can also be emotional, as in the strategy for the trial. Find him innocent because of his looks and his ethnicity. There may be a number of reasons why but they should all build to a single thrust—the key thought.

Prove this strategy to yourself. Many of you probably use it or parts of it automatically but these five questions may fill in some holes. Think back to some of the problems you've had recently and apply the five questions. See if the results are the same as what you actually arrived at. Or if, by using the strategy, they would have been better. More imaginative. And maybe even more effective.

To stimulate your thinking in the use of this strategic approach, here are some areas where it has proved effective:

To get a point of view across to a daughter on her choice of college.

Memo to management on why and how the company should encourage and promote daily exercise among its employees.

Plan for an active uncle on what to do in retirement years.

After-dinner speech to the Rotary Club stressing the need for community help in downtown beautification.

Character motivation in a movie script. In Scene 32 what is Miss Moneypenny's perception of James Bond? What do we want her to do? What is the key thought or action that will get her to do what we want her to do? What logic or emotion is there in this action that will get her to act on the key thought? Screenwriters use variations of the strategic approach automatically. But when you're stuck, it often helps to go through the five steps consciously.

General and abstract ideas are the source of the greatest errors of mankind.
—Rousseau, *Émile*

The fact is that this process, or a modification of it, can help stimulate the right side to overcome creative blocks, channel thoughts, logic, direction, or persuasion in almost every project or problem. If you remember nothing else from this book, remember the five questions.

Fine for commercials, plays, movies, inventions, stories, but how do you visualize when you're writing a letter or an announcement or something that seemingly is all words? First, don't visualize the words unless they themselves are a part of a picture. (Sign on trash can: "DROP DEAD fish and other garbage in this container. Keep Brickton Clean." You get the idea. Giant lettering for the first two words with the rest of it in tiny typeface so that the only thing you see from a distance is DROP DEAD.)

Rather than visualize the words, try to imagine the faces of your audience or readers and the reaction you'd like to get from them. Let that help lead you to your creative approach. Do you want to make them smile or challenge them or reassure them or scare them or wake them up? All of these, by the way, have to do with the creative format I presented on page 48. What we want to accomplish is the answer to Question Three, "What do we want our audience to do?" What we're talking about here is how we accomplish it. And arriving at this choice, or even developing the number of choices that we have, can be better done through visualization.

There is a way to get your right side in the mood to do this. Next time you read the paper, try to picture every story that you read. All of them. Not too hard to see something on the screen in your head when you read about riots in Manila or a towering home run in the Kingdom or hanky-panky in a congressman's office. But what about the story announcing that Brazil had stopped interest on its foreign loans or telling about the judge who was sent a poisoned candy valentine? Aha. As I mention this you see shocked bankers on Wall Street looking at teletypes and holding their heads or the judge opening the box of candy and muttering to his wife, "Hmmm. Wonder who this is from." He looks puzzled at the card, which says "To My Valentine" as his wife samples a piece and says, "That's funny. Good candy though . . . arggghhh."

chapter 12

BEFORE YOU START, GET THE BIG PICTURE

Whether we're lying in bed, concentrating in a research lab, or hunching over a word processor, creative solutions often come into awareness in the form of images, according to Willis Harman and Howard Rheingold in their book *Higher Creativity*. And this seems to me to be good because the solution in its entirety appears on the screen in the front of your mind. Not just parts or words but the whole thing. The big picture. Most of the time. But not always.

To help achieve this end, it seems to me that if you can train yourself to think visually from the beginning you can, perhaps, nudge the subconscious in the right direction. You would think that this would be easy in creating TV commercials but you'd be surprised at the number of people who attack the challenge with slogans or jingles and beautifully crafted words. I urge them to wed the idea to a visual concept.

When the classic commercial for Wendy's hamburgers was in the concept stage no one said, "Hey. I have an idea, let's have someone ask 'Where's the beef?'" The copywriter visualized three elderly ladies listening to the claims of competitors for all the accoutrements their hamburgers had while they examined the products. He started the dialogue as they exclaimed over the claims ("big, fluffy bun") and then it seemed a natural step for one, after seeing the less than large amount of meat on the big, fluffy bun, to look up and ask in that wonderful gravelly voice, "Where's the beef?" That memorable line grew out of a visualization of the complete scene, not just words.

chapter 13

USING ANXIETY

For some people anxiety and fear can be a creative kick in the pants. Nothing like, "I wonder what'll happen if I don't get this done" to help get things done. But for most, any kind of anxiety can cause the big clutch. Or at least a small dam in the flow of creative thoughts. Therefore it is nice if you can find ways to put anxiety somewhere else and enter the altered state unencumbered.

I find it helpful to take steps in solving whatever is preying on my mind before tackling a creative task. Notice I said take steps. Not solve it, necessarily. But make some moves in the right direction. If the thought of organizing everything for the preparation of your income tax is hanging over your head, spend some time getting things organized. If you can't really think straight because you've got a heavy schedule of things to do, sit down and work out an hour-by-hour plan. Whether or not it's right or you actually follow it is not important. Your objective is to lessen impedimental anxiety.

Of course, there are those high or higher anxieties that can't be brushed off with a few hours of organization. And I'm not talking about things that require professional help but rather everyday worries that we all have. This calls for a somewhat philosophic approach. In many cases the act of creating can be its own antidote, particularly if you use the creative act as therapeutic relaxation. On the other hand, if the right side is about to be engaged in some heavy output you may want to prepare it for the relaxed state.

1. Practice not letting your anxieties or temperament take charge. If you're stuck in a traffic jam, program yourself to sit back and relax. Let your imagination roll along.

Play the observation game of the people in the cars around you. Who are they? Where are they going? Are they upset over the jam? If you carry the small pad, jot down notes or thoughts on things completely apart from what you're doing (which is trying not to get angry or frustrated). Write some poetry. Or the lyrics of a song. Or just dream. See if you can remember where you were and what you were doing ten years ago. Now, if you can accomplish pushing your anxieties to the rear of everything in these moments of frustration, you'll find it easier and easier to do all of the time. And soon you may be able to move them away from your creative concentration almost on command.

2. If you can afford the time, try to allow a period for decompression before you put the right side to work. Sit and read or listen to music. You're trying to enter the altered state through relaxation. Much has been written about meditation and Yoga and various other transcendental approaches to this problem. No more will be written here as it is too large and profound a subject to be covered in short bursts. However, it is well worth looking into for those who are searching for different ways to go beyond the ordinary experience.

3. Finally, one of the best ways to lessen anxieties is to talk with someone. Even if nothing is resolved, the weight seems to be lifted from the shoulders through a process of transference. And the listener, and receiver, also feels good because just by listening he or she has helped, and may even give more help with advice. Of course, you have to be ready to accept the fact that perhaps the advice is (1) not good, (2) goes against what you thought, and (3) thus may heighten your anxiety. That's why, when deciding to talk to someone, be selective. Look for the known soother. Remember, you're not searching for solutions. Just a less anxious state of mind.

In his old age Brahms announced to his friends that he was going to stop composing music and enjoy the time left to him. Several months went by without Brahms writing a note. But there came the day when a new Brahms composition made its debut. "I thought you weren't going to write anymore," a friend reminded him. "I wasn't," said the composer, "but after a few days away from it I was so happy at the thought of no more writing that the music came to me without effort."

chapter 14

ON ZIGGING AGAINST DEADLINES

One of the thrills of being creative, of finding that "My God, there is something working in the right side of my brain," is that sooner or later something is done about it. A painting comes forth. An engineering problem is solved. A poem is created. And believe it or not, "they" liked it. And if the magic rewards of published works or art showings or new product ideas or inventions or musical arrangements or scientific breakthroughs do become a reality, deadlines become equally real. And they have to be coped with.

The professional knows all of this. She realizes that when she turns in a story outline and the editor says, "Pat, that's terrific. I'll have the contract in the morning. But I'd like to get it in the next issue. Can you wrap it up for me in two weeks?" she's got trouble. But at least she has an idea and an outline to build on. It's not like the playwright who, overnight, has to come up with a whole new scene in the third act because, "I dunno, Harry, it's just not making it the way it is. Why don't you have a couple of pops after dinner and see if you can dream up something?"

Or the copywriter who picks up the phone and hears, "Stanley, big trubello. Client bent over and retched at your campaign idea. Honest. I thought he was gonna bespoil his wastebasket. Get the six o'clock out here and see if you can dream up something on the plane. We've got a meeting to show it to him first thing in the A.M." Terrific. Why is it that the left-siders always think that the right-siders can "dream up something" any time, any place. It's because that's the

> It is not learning, grace nor gear, Nor easy meat and drink, But bitter pinch of pain and fear, That makes creation think.
> —Rudyard Kipling, *The Benefactors*

professional's job. And so the successful ones learn how to cope.

The reason for all of this is that the amateur and especially the budding pro must learn this art as well, and just because their livelihood may not be dependent on their extracurricular creativity, they often don't take deadlines seriously. And thus, too often, the following may be heard:

> "An editor from Random House liked it. Matter of fact, she asked me to do some things and said she wanted to look at it again in three weeks or so—but I haven't had time."
>
> "Guy from Washington says he's never seen anything like it. Suggests I check out the patents. But I dunno—that's a lot of work, and I've got enough to do in my regular job."
>
> "The creative director needs a new concept on Monday. I told him that my family's coming home for the weekend. Something that can't be changed and I've already made all the plans. So I asked if he could get someone else."

Here is where you've got to listen to the discipline of the left side of the brain to help you get the job done. And it will go something like this:

1. Because fear sometimes leads to procrastination or creative paralysis, it will induce you not to be scared of the task. You can do it because you wouldn't have gotten as far as you have, you wouldn't have produced what they liked, you wouldn't have the job they hired you for if you didn't have the ability.

2. From the moment the deadline is given, the left side will go into action replanning your schedule. It will pump adrenalin into one of its subsections to get it to organize the materials you need. (If you're going on a plane, let's get a folder of your notes, copies of reference material, pencils or portable typewriter or tape recorder, and legal pad or sketchbook.) Another subsection will shorten the time you are taking for certain tasks, will tell voice to make phone calls to cancel or postpone nonessential meetings and appointments to allow time for the right side to do its job.

3. It will prepare you for sacrifice by possibly offering compromise. ("Don't sulk. You don't have to give up the Hamptons, dummy. You've got about three hours' work here. Go on out. But take it easy Friday night so you can get up early Saturday morning and go downstairs before everyone gets up and work this thing out over a cup of coffee alone in the kitchen.") If you have to give up the Hamptons, or vacation, or evenings of numbing relaxation at the television set, or a concert, or some good reading, left side will convince you it's for a good cause, or perhaps a financial reward. Even the success of your job. In the latter case, if your future depends on how well you perform your zigging and you're not willing to make some sacrifices, then you're in the wrong place and you might just as well stop here and go along with the rest of the zaggers.

4. At the same time, while the left side is sitting in the command post orchestrating all of this, the right side is performing its own task. It starts the process of sliding ideas into the subconscious. It dumps more thoughts into the pot. It doesn't ask for answers—yet. But actually I've found you can help this automatic subconscious process by consciously thinking about the problem at times when you usually let your mind go blank. While driving to work or the dry cleaners or school. While working out in exercise class or jogging. While sitting on the bus. (At this point, forget about the tip where you try to figure out who the other people are and what they're doing.) Anywhere you're alone.

5. Now the time comes when you've got to get it going. This is the test, the challenge, the opportunity, the key moment, the raison d'être for the right side. And wherever you are, your surroundings are blanked out. You enter

Compromise, if not the spice of life, is its solidity.
—Phyllis McGinley, "Suburbia, of Thee I Sing," *The Province of the Heart*

Hi ho, hi ho—it's off to work we go . . .
—Happy, Dopey, Sleepy, Grumpy, Sneezy, Bashful, Doc

57

the altered state. You are completely absorbed in giving birth to a solution to the challenge. You've prepared yourself with materials, time, and, most important, prethinking in the subconscious. But now you must use your skills—logic, simplification, and your sleeping creative ability, which is now wide awake—to come up with the answer.

chapter 15

STIMULUS I: HOW TO START ZIGGING

Books have been written on the subject, but I've found that one of the most basic and practical ways to get things going can be illustrated by the following incident that happened about two weeks after I'd started my first job in the advertising department of the Armstrong Cork Company (now Armstrong World Industries) forty years ago. I was given one of their famous national magazine ads and asked to do another ad for the same product. I looked at the format, kept the feeling of it but suggested the picture be placed at the bottom of the ad rather than the top. Then I changed the headline slightly and proudly presented the results to E. Cameron Hawley, the then advertising manager and later best-selling author of such books as *Executive Suite* and *Cash McCall*. The conversation that took place, more or less, is as follows:

> **HAWLEY:** What the hell is this?
>
> **ME:** Ummmmm-er. It's the ad you asked me to do. As you see I've kept it in the same format.
>
> **HAWLEY:** Yes. You've changed a couple of words and slightly rearranged the picture. Is that what you call creative?
>
> **ME:** Uh . . . no sir.
>
> **HAWLEY:** Then why the hell did you do it?
>
> **ME:** Ulp.
>
> **HAWLEY:** Come back tomorrow at eight (which was Saturday. We worked in those days.)

ME: Right.

HAWLEY: . . . and I want to see the headline done 50 different ways.

ME: Fifty! I don't think there are 50 different ways.

HAWLEY: If you want to be a creative copywriter, you'll find 50 different ways.

He forced me to think, to try it, to reach, to experience. It was the real beginning of the unlocking of the right side of my brain . . . of exploring the path of zigdom.

Try it yourself. Next time you write a personal letter, write it the way you normally would. Then do it again, trying to be completely different, but still with the same basic thoughts. Then push yourself and do it once more. You'll begin to probe for different approaches. You may find that the basic information you're giving doesn't lend itself to a variety of creative approaches. You may question the information. Whether or not it's raining as you write may not warrant a paragraph rather than a few words. Remember, creativity is not measured by length. "Dear Ib. As I write this it's raining" certainly is more succinct than "Dear Ib. At the moment columns of water are coursing down the windowpane, splashing off the sill and forming rivulets that find their way down the sidewalk and cascade over the curb into the ever-growing stream in the gutter." On the other hand, knowing your audience is important. Ib may like that kind of stuff.

Right, you say. Ib likes to visualize her old house when I write. OK, try it again. "Dear Ib. It's raining and dripping off the leaves of the big lilac bush in the front yard where we hid when we didn't want Mom to find us. The water's running down the sidewalk and over the same cracks where we used to have our hopscotch games. Watching it made me think of you and inspired me to write." Not bad. At least you're getting in the swing of trying different approaches. And, as I said, that's one of the first steps in being creative.

Having imagination, it takes you an hour to write a paragraph that, if you were unimaginative, would take you only a minute. Or you might not write the paragraph at all.
—Franklin P. Adams, *Half a Loaf*

In good writing, words become one with things.
—Emerson, *Journals*

Eventually you'll automatically search for different ways before you start or as you form the construction in your mind. You'll reject, at least for the time being, the obvious. And when you come across one of your letters in Ib's desk, you won't be embarrassed and say, "How could I write such junk?" You might even say, "Hey, I remember that letter. That's when I discovered that I really am creative."

I touched on keeping a daily journal earlier. This exercise can also help develop the zigging instinct. But be as specific as possible. If you've never done anything like this, start with a description of the scene around you. Where is it? What are the colors, textures, smells? Are there people involved? What do they look like? What are they wearing? Do they gesture as they talk? Are they active? How do they move? What do they say? Can you write their dialogue phonetically? In what I thought was a hilarious scene in a movie, whose title escapes me, a very nice lady from Texas is telling her friend, a geologist from the North, that to get ahead in Midland she had to learn how to "talk Texas." Went something like this.

> "What business are you in?"
> "The oil business."
> "No, awl—not oil. Awl."
> "I'm in the awl business."
> "That's it. But it's bid. B-i-d."
> "Bid?"
> "Yup . . . bidness . . . not bizness."
> "Ahm in the awl bidness."
> "Yeah. Now you're talkin' Texas."

Now do what Hawley asked me to do. Make two columns on a page. In the first column, put the first descriptive sentence of your journal of observations. In the other col-

> I wish to write such rhymes as shall not suggest a restraint, but contrariwise the wildest freedom.
>
> —Ralph Waldo Emerson, *Journal*

umn search for a way to say it differently. Reach out and zig.

COLUMN 1	COLUMN 2
The plane was coming in for a landing at Minneapolis.	I saw the tiny white farmhouses around Minneapolis begin to sprout details—a man walking from a tractor to the back door, a dog barking silently on a front porch.
The roads wound through the fields with tiny cars scooting along.	The cars looked like different-colored bugs crawling on winding brown ribbons.
Water tanks seemed to stand out from the rest of the buildings.	White water tanks were mushrooms growing at the edge of each town.

And so forth. This type of exercise forces you to look at things differently. You get rid of the obvious first. And then you begin to stimulate creativity. Simple, challenging, difficult, but almost always effective. What you're doing is stepping over or around or through the guidelines of the obvious. And sometimes those guidelines aren't guidelines at all. They're habit. You do things the same way because it's easier. But no one said being creative was easy. Of course, in trying to be different you must be careful that after a while you don't fall into a pattern, because if you do, zigging turns into zagging.

chapter 16

STIMULUS II: EXCITING THE RIGHT SIDE

How do you get the right side excited? One way is to look at and experience what other people have done in the field you're interested in. Surround yourself with greatness. Read. Go to galleries, museums, films. Do some research. Try to figure out the thinking pattern of the people who are experts in your particular field. Now, all of this assumes that you have a working knowledge or talent for what you want to do. You've done some writing. You know some of the rhythms and structure of poetry; chord progression is not unfamiliar. You know how to experiment with a wet wash on watercolor paper. The reading and research will build on this knowledge.

If you're a writer, for example, you'll begin to notice technique as well as content. You'll read and reread sections that are different, appealing, intriguing. If you're an embryonic artist, you'll spend time eight or ten inches from a Van Gogh or Andrew Wyeth looking and marveling at brush strokes and color blending. With Miró or Mondrian you may step back and try to figure out color composition. Why the artist suddenly used a block of yellow in the lower left. Is it balanced by something in the upper right? Is it there to change a point of view? Is it pleasing? Distracting? Emotional? Or is it there so that people will look and say, "Why is it there?" What was the artist thinking of? Why did he do it? Should I try something like that in the next thing I do? Perhaps the vase and flowers that I was going to paint don't have to be centered. Or if they're off center, perhaps they don't have to have a piece of drapery on the other side to balance them. I think I'll make some quick rough sketches or loose watercolors to see how it looks.

In addition, talk to people who inspire and/or stimulate you. They may be experts in your field—other writers or artists or people with imagination. Or they may just be friends who get you to think, who unconsciously goad you on. If they are experts, then of course you can use them for advice on approaches, techniques, ways to channel your thinking.

All of this is fine if, as I mentioned, you have some rudimentary knowledge of what you're doing. But what about the person who feels she has some zigging ability locked in the right side but doesn't know how or has never tried to coax it out? We talk about the people who can't stop being creative. Who seem to bubble over with the stuff. Perhaps it spins around going nowhere once it's unleashed. But it does flow out almost constantly. Most reluctant ziggers, however, keep their talents locked up because they're lazy or procrastinators or have an excessively dominant left side. The fact is, they really don't know how to encourage and build on their talents. These are the people who must do two things:

> Genius is 1% inspiration and 99% perspiration.
> —**Thomas Alva Edison,** *Life*

1. Resolve to do something about it. Very important. You've got to get over procrastinating. To get things going, as was said before, you've got to set some creative time. You can be encouraged by friends, family, even this book. But somewhere along the line you've got to take hold and act.

> Medicine, to produce health, has to examine disease, and music, to create harmony, must investigate discord.
> —**Plutarch,** *Lives*

2. Learn. Learn the basics of your chosen creative craft. And this means more than going to galleries or movies. You can't zig until you know what you're zigging from. To go against the grain you've got to know which way the grain is going. This may mean courses. And there are many available at convenient hours or on weekends almost everywhere. At least in most of the creative fields we're talking about. I'm not sure that you can pick up a course on the art of bonsai at the drop of a pair of clippers, but who knows? But if courses are impossible, then read. Instructional books are great for course augmentation. And they can also help on their own. Of course the books have a harder time giving you something a good teacher has to offer—stimulation and encouragement. Even experienced people never stop learning. Naomi Blivens, *The New Yorker* writer, read 15 books on World War II before preparing her review of David Eisenhower's book on his grandfather.

The pros know that another reason for learning a craft is security. It's a very comforting feeling to realize, for example, that you can fall back on portrait work or a landscape or a jingle for a commercial to keep things going while you're exploring some exciting new creative frontiers. David Hockney worries about the artists who approach their work narrowly and specialize in only one technique, often without even learning the basics of drawing. While there are a number of good rock groups that grew out of the 60s there are more bad ones that failed. I contend that one of the reasons is that the participants weren't really musicians. They hadn't learned the basics. Drummers proliferated who hadn't the slightest idea of how to execute a press roll or paradiddle or basic five or seven roll. They didn't even know how to hold the sticks. They gripped them like hammers. But that was all right because the music they played was right out of the boom-da-da school. There was no need to learn anything else. Same rhythm pattern for everything. And same chord structure. Learn four guitar chords and you were in business. Then turn up the amps and blast away. If you hit a wrong chord the distortion was so great that no one could tell anyway.

The artist Lee Savage is a classic example of how knowing the basics can support creative exploration. To keep things going he worked at J. Walter Thompson, the advertising agency, as an art director specializing in TV story boards. But he yearned to spend more time doing serious

Nothing will come of nothing.
  —**Shakespeare,** *King Lear*

painting. So he toiled away, hoping to save enough money to be able to take off and just paint. One day he was working at the drawing board when someone from the treasurer's office approached him and, as Lee reported it, the conversation went something like this:

MAN: Lee Savage?

LEE: (not looking up) Yup.

MAN: Here's an accounting of your profit sharing for the year.

LEE: How much?

MAN: You have accumulated $18,000.

LEE: (looking up suddenly) $18,000!!!

MAN: As of the end of last mo—

LEE: Where is it, for God's sake?

MAN: Why it's invested in our profit shar—

LEE: Well, give it to me. I want it.

MAN: You don't understand. You can't get it until you leave the company.

LEE: I have to quit to get it?

MAN: That's right.

LEE: I quit. Let's go get it.

And he did. And took the money and went to England and painted until it ran out. Then he took a job with J. Walter Thompson's London office and earned some more. (He was so talented that the company welcomed him back, even on this more or less sporadic basis.) Lee worked this way for some time until his fine art began to pay off.

Now, aside from teaching you how to do it, the instructional mode should also make you want to do it. The right side, as it gets some instruction, keeps saying, "Wow. This is great. Let me try it. Let me take a crack at it. Let's go." The instructional period should also make you curious and inquisitive. And this leads to the aforementioned gallery/museum/movie adventures.

Professional ziggers, without thinking about it or even realizing it, have this proven to them regularly. In an advertising agency a creative team is assigned the advertising for a financial institution. Incidentally, one of the best stimulators in cases like this is to make the creative team feel that the assignment is a responsibility. The financial institution is their account. They are charged with coming up with compelling advertising for it. They are not asked to "give a hand" or "see what you can do." They are told it's their baby. And that in itself is a nice stimulus.

But when the assignment first comes through, they may sigh a bit. "Why couldn't we have gotten the beer account where we could have some fun with the advertising? Financial advertising is deadly, boring. And I don't even understand it." But after a few days of briefing and listening to client enthusiasm and reading research and competitive facts and helping to develop direction and strategy, the creative team begins to develop some expertise—and opinions and ideas. And when someone says, "You have my sympathy, working on that financial stuff," you hear, "Whadya mean? I gotta helluva'n idea. We found out that we have a big advantage over banks on our secured loans. We can give 'em a loan in as little as 24 hours. Usually takes a bank weeks. And we have people ready to OK it any time. So I want to do a simple side-by-side. On one side, Mr. Smith is going to a bank on a Saturday morning. He's welcomed through the locked plate-glass door by the cleaning woman. On the other side of the screen, Mr. Jones goes to our place and is welcomed by the manager who's there on a Saturday morning. Big smile. Ready to do business . . ."

All of this instruction and inspiration is fine for creative activity in the arts. But what, you ask, about the people who want to unleash some zigging in the field of engineering or medicine or accounting? Read on, friend.

chapter 17

STIMULUS III: A GUIDE FOR THE WORLD'S LEFT SIDES—ENGINEERS, ACCOUNTANTS, AND SO FORTH

The left-siders, as we mentioned before, are those people whose left side of the brain dominates. These are people who use logic, sequential reasoning. They reach conclusions by linking their thoughts together in a linear procession. They base many of their decisions on facts. To get them to zig we must somehow sublimate the left side and develop the right side.

Now, for some this might be done through logic. The left side can accept thinking the opposite. It's concrete, not abstract. The opposite of up is down, of tall is short, of wet is dry. Fine. But so what, says Lefty. What's the conclusion? Where do we go from here?

RIGHT SIDE: Well . . . it's just an exercise to get thinking differently. We try to draw some conclusions.

LEFT SIDE: What conclusions?

RIGHT SIDE: Uh . . . try this. Trees grow up, right?

LEFT SIDE: (getting impatient) Yeah.

RIGHT SIDE: What's the opposite?

LEFT SIDE: Trees grow down? This is silly.

Pure logic is the ruin of the spirit.
—Saint-Exupéry, *Flight to Avras*

RIGHT SIDE: OK . . . what's the conclusion?

LEFT SIDE: I dunno what the hell you're talking about.

RIGHT SIDE: If trees grow down, what happens?

LEFT SIDE: (exasperated) For God's sake, I don't know.

RIGHT SIDE: You'd have a lot more forests in China.

LEFT SIDE: (throwing hands in the air hopelessly) I resign!

Logic. The art of thinking and reasoning in strict accordance with the limitations and incapacities of the human misunderstanding.
—Ambrose Bierce, *The Devil's Dictionary*

However, in a left-side-dominated brain it's often difficult to use this kind of logic to make the switch from left to right because the left is too dominant. It refuses to listen or rather it refuses to accept. Kind of a "Catch 22" situation. Use logic to arrive at a conclusion that's not logical. But to do that you must use silly logic, which can't be done because it's no longer logical to the dominant left side.

So another method must be found to move thinking into the right side. One of the best and most unusual and most interesting ways is the device that Betty Edwards describes in her book *Drawing on the Right Side of the Brain*. Essentially she asks the strong left-sider to take a simple line drawing of a face. (She uses Picasso's "Portrait of Igor Stravinsky" as an example.) The subject is to look at it and follow the lines with the eye, naming each feature in sequence—hair, forehead, eyes, nose, etc. Then draw it without taking the pencil off the paper.

Next the picture is to be turned upside down and the drawing done again but this time without naming the features. The fact is the features are hard to recognize upside down so the mind concentrates on the line alone and right side begins to take over.

LEFT SIDE: Okay, let's start at the top. I guess that must be the hair. No, it's upside down, so it's the leg . . . or a piece of the chair . . . or . . . I dunno.

RIGHT SIDE: Let's just follow the line. It goes down straight and another curved line cuts into it about three-quarters of the way down and then circles back down . . .

LEFT SIDE: I don't know what we're drawing.

RIGHT SIDE: I don't care what we're drawing. I'm just following the line with my *eye* and making my hand do what I tell it . . . two more short straight lines going into a shallow oval running at right angles . . .

LEFT SIDE: This is boring.

RIGHT SIDE: . . . then another curved line running across the . . .

LEFT SIDE: I wish you'd get off this so that we could do something useful . . . (mutters)

See what's happening? What was originally a recognizable drawing of a man is now an abstract adventure. And because it's abstract and not logical, the left side doesn't want to cope with it. Left side wants to get on with something logical, understandable—with whatever is next. But it can't because the right side *is now becoming dominant.* Right side doesn't hear or care about left side. It's involved completely in the drawing, concentrating on the picture, the hand, and the line. It is becoming one with the creative process.

And that is what we're trying to accomplish.

Now, when you're finished turn the drawing upside down and compare it with the original copy done by left side from the right-side-up picture—you'll be amazed.

RIGHT SIDE: Wow. Look at that! Pretty good. Much better than the first one.

LEFT SIDE: I don't believe it. I don't understand it.

RIGHT SIDE: We're talkin' creativity, kid. Something you'll never understand.

LEFT SIDE: But . . . but . . . it's not logical.

What's happened is that the left side, to quote Betty Edwards " . . . confused and blocked by the unfamiliar image and unable to name or symbolize as usual, turned off, and the job passed over to the right hemisphere. Perfect!" And because the right side is more suited to even this creative task of concentrating and copying it does it well, and has fun doing it.

This is fine if you want to get in the right-side mode for drawing or painting. But what about those of us who would like to write or compose or practice the art of Japanese flower arranging. Are there ways to block the left side without turning everything upside down? I think so. At least I've used two.

The first is the very popular practice of wiping the brain clean—both sides. It's done a number of ways. Meditation. Relaxation. Certain activities that become automatic and induce boredom. The theory is that as thoughts drift off and away and the left and right sides slip into a relaxed stupor, the subconscious, which seems to be always puttering away at an unconscious level, begins to surface because there's nothing blocking it. And as its thoughts and ideas percolate, the right side wakes up and begins to work them over.

With me, this happens when I'm jogging at dawn. But don't make the mistake of thinking that all forms of exercise can induce this boredom and resultant brain clearing. If you try it when you're playing tennis, for instance, you'll automatically lose that all-important concentration and the game will suffer. OK, if you don't care—but most tennis players do, passionately. Even an exercise class is not good if you're supposed to constantly think of what muscles to use. But rowing or swimming or ice skating or even cross-country skiing on a flat course are good boredom stimulants—any activity where you've trained your muscles to give an automatic response.

The second method used is an offshoot of the spontaneity exercise we described on page 22. It's called word association, and like the upside down drawing it works on building up the right side by boring the left. If you have a

When your Daemon is in charge, do not try to think consciously. Drift, wait, and obey.
—Rudyard Kipling, *Something of Myself for My Friends Known and Unknown*

creative challenge that's hard to get started on, begin by writing down words that may be closely or even remotely associated with the project. In the aforementioned campaign for McGruff, the crime dog, I used this as a part of the incubation process that night in the Kansas City airport. I was listing all of the words associated with different animals that might have to do with defeating crime. Roar at crime (lion). Claw crime (tiger). Kick crime (mule). Jump on crime (rabbit). Crush crime (elephant). And so forth—all words that had to do with oblitering the problem. None seemed right. So I went back and rechecked the strategy, the road map to where I should be going. And the public belief or perception about crime gave me my clue.

Because people felt that there's nothing that can be done to defeat crime, all of these powerful crushing, kicking, roaring words were wrong. What we should have been aiming for was something that the public could believe. Doing little things to help protect themselves and make it tougher for a crime to happen. If everyone did these little things they might mount up and help lower the crime rate. Not eliminate it, but lessen it. Words. Nibble. Mouse. Mouse? A mouse as a spokesperson against crime? Huh! Chew. Chew on crime. Sounds like a dog food. Dog. Bark. Bark at crime. Whine at crime. Pee on crime. Bite crime. Hey. Bite on crime. Take a bite out of crime. Hey hey. HELP TAKE A BITE OUT OF CRIME. Eureka!

In addition to helping move into the right-side mode, here word association was used to stimulate the development of an executional device. This is probably its most accepted use. In writing the lyrics for a song or jingle or even in poetry, word association can be a help. In descriptive passages in any kind of writing it can take us away from the ordinary. The moon sparkled on the dark river. Shimmered. Glistened. Rippled. Ripples of light. Paths of light. The moonlight on the river was a rippling path of gold. Trail. As the moon rose it created a rippling trail of gold across the water. Rippling. Dancing. Walking. Undulating. The river glistened as a trail of gold walked to the moon.

But its less-used application may be in opening up new approaches and areas of thought or to help focus a point of view. An example. In the rotisserie restaurant of a few pages back, you've used strategy to delineate your audience and the single-minded appeal, outdoor cooking indoors, that's going to get them to try you. The problem: A description that will project the aura, ambiance, and feeling of the place for use in (1) possibly the name, (2) the decor and marketing, (3) the prospectus for getting the backing. Now, list all of the words that might have something to do with the restaurant. Rotisserie. Grill. Flame. Warm. Meat. Prime. Chops. English. Country. Farm. Kitchen. Rural. New England. Vermont. Barn. Glow. Golden. Toast. Charcoal. Mesquite. Embers. Broiler. Spit. Roasting. Barbecue. In dealing with anything of this sort particular care should be taken as to how the descriptive words are interpreted by the prospective audience. Is rotisserie meaningful in the Midwest? (Remember, we're talking about opening up new areas of thought or focusing a point of view.) What does "chops" mean? Does New England connote a special menu? What are the implications of "country" and "kitchen"?

At first you might decide to build everything around the word "rotisserie" until you find that it has an unwanted French connotation. "Chops" has a nice feel—but there is a worry that it means only pork chops in this area. In the Midwest there is a mystique about New England, and it does not seem to be too restrictive to the menu. Both "country" and "kitchen" project an informality that goes against the price range and the audience we're appealing to. "Charcoal" and "mesquite." Aha. They both bring images of tasty, outdoor grilled meat. Right on strategy. The Mesquite Rotisserie.

Because mesquite is indigenous to the Southwest this becomes the theme for the decor, the signage, advertising, menus, everything. And it was all stimulated by the word-association process. It doesn't always work—at least not the way you might expect it to. But you'll be surprised at how it can open your right side's imagination.

chapter 18

STIMULUS IV: DEVELOPING NEW PRODUCTS, GETTING NEW IDEAS

So far we've been concentrating on zigging in the arts as though it were the special province of professional, budding, or would-be writers, artists, actors, musicians. But one of the most electrifying and rewarding opportunities for creativity is in the development of ideas that give birth to new products, services, or inventions. A good friend of mine, Martin Friedman, who chronicles the birth and sometimes demise of new products for the *DFS New Product News*, suggests the following prerequisites to any kind of new idea or new product development. (The editorial comments are mine.)

1. *Make Sure That There's a Need for It Now or in the Foreseeable Future.* Dr. Lydia Bronte, a consultant to the Carnegie Foundation, has just finished a study on aging in America. Using some of her findings, we're reaching some conclusions on what this will mean to marketers 15 to 20 years from now. And because the baby boomers will be moving into what we call the retirement years but what, in fact, will be their older-active or second-career years, opportunities for different services and products to satisfy the new needs of this unique and large segment of our population will be staggering. Clothes, for example, will be designed more for practicality, which will mean less use of high-heeled shoes. For winter wear will there be a demand for

Henry Ford once called in an efficiency expert to examine the running of his company. The expert made a favorable report, but had reservations about one employee. "It's that man down the corridor," he said. "Every time I go by his office he's just sitting there with his feet on the desk. He's wasting your money." "That man," replied Ford, "once had an idea that saved us millions of dollars. At the time, I believe his feet were planted right where they are now."

lightweight electrically heated outerwear run by a compact long-lasting energy pack carried in the pocket? This is where the left side can take over and help. It's not enough to think that there's a need. You've got to know it. Do some research. Don't let the right side play the reverse role and try to push the idea through with overwhelming enthusiasm. Look for hidden problems. And if there are some, try to solve them. But if they persist, be wary. You can't afford to ignore them. The Edsel failed because the Ford Motor Company was determined to market a car for which there was no need or demand. Every year new beers are introduced in this country and are marketed on image and emotion because there's no rationale for another beer. They fail. On the other hand, Bartles and Jaymes is succeeding not only because of its brilliant advertising but also because it is fulfilling a need in a new and growing category—wine coolers.

Defeat is a fact and victory can be a fact. If the idea is good, it will survive defeat, it may even survive the victory.
—Stephen Vincent Benét, *John Brown's Body*

The marketing of a typewriter ribbon that can be installed without the usual carbon-smudged fingers would have been terrific 25 years ago but not now. With the proliferation of electronic typewriters and computers, the ribbon is going the way of the two-man tree saw, tire chains, the girdle, and black and white TV. If you have a solution looking for a problem and can't find one, don't waste your time or money. Go on to something else.

2. *Make Sure That No One Else Has Thought of Your Idea or Has Already Marketed It Unless You Can Produce Yours Better or Cheaper or Both.* Automobiles have been around for over a century but in the last ten years Japanese cars have established a niche here not because they're different but rather because they're better and have been less expensive. According to Friedman, in 1985 7,214 new products were introduced in food and drug stores. About 75% of them were similar to other new products. Less than 1% achieved the accepted national success rate of 25 to 35 million dollars a year. Remember, once something has been presented to the public, the idea is no longer new.

3. *Make Sure That It's Practical.* Is the cost prohibitive? Can it be produced in quantities that will fulfill the need? Will mass production change the concept or quality? Even experienced, sophisticated marketers can miss this requirement. Some years ago Life Savers candy developed in its pilot plant a gum with the delicious taste of Life Savers roll candy. The stuff done in the labs and pilot plants was absolutely delicious. No other gum like it. So with fanfare and hoopla and a massive advertising campaign, the product was introduced and got great initial trial. But that was all. No one came back for seconds because no matter how hard they tried (and believe me they did) the company could not mass produce the same delightful flavor they'd developed in the lab and pilot plant. Perhaps, someday, they'll solve the problem. If so, I intend to be the first in line to buy some. And I'm not even a gum nut.

4. *Make Sure You Can Get Your Product or Idea Before the Public.* Good ideas, these days, usually make it. But not always. There is an abundance of tragic failures where an idea is stillborn because of various unforeseen or overlooked obstacles in the marketplace. And they can't be eliminated if you don't recognize them—preferably in advance. My father once invented a plant-food-fertilizer called Char-Gro. Much better than anything on the market then because it used a charcoal base to hold the water next to the roots. He tested it in a number of areas. On our own front lawn one half was treated with Char-Gro, the other with the competition. The Char-Gro half grew so fast and long it looked obscene. But it ultimately failed because he didn't have a strong distribution system or marketing muscle (translation: money). He got the stuff into a number of garden stores in upstate New York at a competitive price. But the big chemical companies, which were well entrenched with their plant foods and had plenty of money to do it, cut their prices, undersold Char-Gro, took their losses until they'd driven Dad's product out of the market. Since then I've used only horse and cow effluent on my garden.

The only sure weapon against bad ideas is better ideas.
—Whitney Griswold, *New York Times*

5. *When You've Looked for All of the Problems and Supposedly Solved Them—Look Again.* Look for hidden booby traps. Ask others to look. Get some dispassionate, neutral potential users of your ideas to review it. And if there's trouble, don't look the other way. Don't brush them off because you've sold yourself on the idea. Malcolm Land, the brother of the inventor of the Polaroid camera and a brilliant scientist and entrepeneur in his own right, once told me, while I was trying to overlook a problem in the development of a new motor oil (it ruined an advertising idea I had), "You can fool thy brother, thy sister, and thy mother—but never, never try to fool thyself." Only he used the vernacular.

chapter 19

STIMULUS V: THE GROUP THINK

So far we've talked about getting your right side in the mood to do something as an individual effort. But often creativity becomes a group engagement. You're developing an approach for a home-made videotape presentation with your town's zoning board concerning a proposed zoning change. You're working with a committee to put together an original "review" for your PTA. You're formulating, with the members of your board, a grant proposal for an existing family crisis center. In any case when you're trying to develop ideas with a group of people, you should know something about group dynamics and their ever elusive, sometimes obdurate, often shy, constantly ego-driven, hopefully cooperative, prayerfully bright right sides. Again, much of what I'll refer to is a combination of common sense and psychology. But stimulating creativity puts a new twist on most everything we do. Hearken.

1. If you're the leader of this proposed ménage, choose people with certain qualities. The aforementioned Chauncey Karten used to tell his classes at the University of Michigan that successful creative people have three qualities: talent, intelligence, motivation. And by talent he meant creative talent. We went into this in another way when we were talking about creativity and intelligence earlier. If you can get some people in your group that have these three qualities, fine. But not all of the people. With that much motivation, mayhem will run the meeting. Actually you can probably do all right if you have people with any two of the three qualities.

If they're talented and motivated, let their instincts take over and you can guide them—with intelligence. If they're intelligent and motivated, use them for strategies, theory, and positioning your approach—but not for creativity. They're probably too left-side oriented to give you much help, anyway. If they're intelligent and talented, but lazy, you must light the firecracker.

2. In looking at these qualities, remember that motivation is the one thing that can be changed. Part of your job in running a group session is to be a leader and to not only motivate but instill motivation in your cohorts. We'll go into this more in the next section.

3. At least one member of the group should have some experience in the area that you're concerned with. Use it as a guide. And be careful that your experienced expert doesn't become the group nay-sayer. ("Nah . . . that's no good. We tried if four years ago and it didn't work then. Why should it work now?") Don't lock yourself into the past. Often this attitude stimulates the left side rather than the right because it's a known. The right side wants to explore the unknown but could be held back by the facts of the past. Let the past be a jumping-off spot for the future. "If it ain't broke, don't fix it" may be a safe philosophy, but it's certainly not a creative one.

4. In selecting your group, make sure that you end up with an odd number so that you'll have a majority and a swing position.

chapter 20

STIMULUS VI: GROUP STIMULATION

As has been mentioned, word association, thought association, and general informal meetings are great ways to stimulate zigging. But there is a more formal way. You may already have used it in one form or another. It's called brainstorming and it was developed some years ago by Alex Osborne, one of the founders of the advertising agency BBDO. Because it is designed to develop a right-side mode through the interaction of a number of people, many of whom may have nothing to do with the creative problem at hand, it can be a very forceful creative stimulus. Simply, it's designed to start with a premise and then create an atmosphere where ideas build on one another. But to make it work there are some very strict guidelines that must be adhered to. Here's how it goes.

1. When this kind of exercise is done professionally, a trained leader is usually in charge. But anyone with a little common sense, an ability to listen, and some experience in group dynamics or running meetings should be able to conduct a session. The first step is to select the participants. And here we may differ a bit from the descriptions of people that we recommended for the general informal meetings in the last section. Selecting an experienced person in the field we're discussing, for example, may not be such a good idea because here we're not necessarily interested in the past. Just ideas. And it's hard for some people to divorce themselves from what they've been doing and take a completely fresh view. Because ideas are what we want, the

He who follows the leader learns to lead the follower.
—G. W. van den Bosch, wise Dutch friend

participants should be heavy right-siders. Their jobs or titles should not enter into the selection. Just their minds. Now, you may think that this means only quick and articulate people. Not necessarily. So that you won't lose the deep-thinking right-siders who may not be top-of-the-mind communicators, there is a special briefing document that will be explained next. The number of participants should not be less than six or more than thirteen.

If the sailors become too numerous, the ship sinks.
—Arab proverb

2. The briefing document should be sent out about two weeks before the session. It should contain all of the pertinent facts related to the project. Everything. Perhaps even a few examples of ideas that have come up to get the participants thinking. But not too many suggestions. I once participated in one of these things where the moderator outlined about 10 answers to each of the problems in the briefing. She looked smart. And I felt dumb. It completely discouraged me from coming up with any ideas. Also include with the briefing document three 3″ × 5″ cards. Each participant is to come to the sessions with three ideas. They will act as starters for many. And for the more thoughtful right-siders mentioned above, they will offer an opportunity to peruse the problem and come up with more complete answers beforehand. The glib, articulate communicators often do not do this, at least not as thoroughly, because they can depend on their deft tongues to pull them through. They'll get their chance to prove themselves in the actual session.

3. The session. The only equipment needed is a tape recorder, pads and pencils, and a basket for the cards. (I always appreciate this. No matter how many times I remind myself, I'm always arriving at meetings patting my pockets to find the lost or forgotten pencil or small pad.) To open, the participants should introduce themselves and their occupations. One good reason for not having too many people from the same organization is the elimination of power politics ("I have a wild idea—but what will she think of it? Maybe it'll get back to so-and-so and I may look foolish. I guess I had better not mention it.")

Next you should very quickly explain the rules—both of them. The first is that no one can say no. No matter how bad or far-fetched or wild an idea or suggestion is, it may stimulate thinking and other ideas that can be built on. And this kind of building is what these sessions are designed to do. The second rule is that each idea be jotted on a 3″ × 5″ card and put into the basket. The ideas can be sorted out later.

Now comes the warm-up, which is designed to eliminate group embarrassment and to begin the transfer from the left-side sequential thinking to the right-side free wheeling. It can consist of nothing more than asking the people some of their likes and dislikes in a field that may or may not be related to the subject of the session. If, for example, you wanted to generate ideas about motor oils you might start the warm-up by asking the participants what their favorite and least favorite cars are and why. Remember, the objective is to get them loose and verbal.

Speaking of verbal, one of the things to watch out for is the over-talking take-over specialist. He delights in taking over the meeting. Your job will be to keep him happily under control so that he doesn't shut off ideas from the others. One way to do this is to set a time limit on the meeting—say two hours—and gently remind him of this after he's gone on too long. Tell him to add his thoughts to the cards. Then, throughout the rest of the meeting keep the ideas from everyone flowing and building. If an idea sparks nothing from anyone (including you), say, "Thank you, that's good. Put it in the basket" and move on quickly to the next idea. But keep things positive. In this kind of session you're a combination moderator, guide, and cheerleader. Toward the end of the two hours pay particular attention to the people who have not said much. They may be the take-their-time right-siders who have been mulling over the ideas that have been flying around them. They may produce great insights.

4. The post-session. This is the sifting through of the ideas, rejecting the impossible, and deciding which of the

Creativity varies inversely with the number of cooks involved in the broth.
—Bernice Fitz-Gibbon, *Macy's, Gimbel's, and Me*

possible should be pursued and developed. In this process you may wish to have the help of someone who has not been involved. He or she may add objectivity (you may be partial to an idea because of the way that it was presented) and also may be stimulated to further development. A final thought: Let the people whose ideas you select for further work know about it. (And thank the others!) Who knows, they may even be spurred to additional heights.

chapter 21

HOW LONG CAN YOU ZIG?

Here we're talking about the actual creative process. The doing it, not the time spent thinking and planning and letting things ferment while you're working at something else. The answer varies according to many factors—how fresh or tired you are, how disciplined, how professional, how interested, and, of course, outside demands on your time. Strangely enough, some people do well when they're tired if what makes them tired is not a creative problem. That may be because they have been using the left side and the right side is still refreshed. Sometimes this brings on a wonderful tired and very relaxed state and things start to flow. On the other hand, if what you're doing demands a lot of heavy thought and concentration, then it's best to tackle the process when you are as fresh and rested as possible. You should also dovetail this whenever possible with the time of day that you feel most creative.

Discipline is usually a function of the left side, and so if lefty is worn out you may find yourself not finishing what you've started or not getting as much done as you'd planned. When I sit down to start working, I find it helps to set a time limit. I'm going to work on the second scene, starting with an outline, for the next two hours without interruption. Then we'll see what happens. And what happens may be that you get so deeply involved, you make the transition to the right-side mode so completely, that you lose track of time and the two hours stretches to three or four without your knowing it. Or you may find that nothing really works. You approach the scene three different ways

> Perhaps nobody ever accomplishes all that he feels lies in him to do; but nearly everyone who tries . . . learns about how far to attempt to spring.
> —Charles Dudley Warner, "Third Study," *Backlog Studies*

No fine work can be done without concentration and self-sacrifice and toil and doubt.
—Max Beerbohm, "Books Within Books," *And Even Now*

Any work looks wonderful to me except the one which I can do.
—Emerson, *Journals*

in the two hours and you're really no further ahead than when you started. Discouraging. It may be because you're tired or preoccupied or not feeling well. But it may also be because you had to go through three varied approaches to get to the one you need, and therefore the two hours is spent wisely. If things are not happening the way you'd like, try to stick it out for the time limit you set; anyway, the "Eureka factor" may even hit in the last five minutes. And then the hour and 55 frustrating minutes of seemingly worthless work will have been worth it.

Professionals, as you can imagine, have to face the problem of time differently. Creativity isn't a welcome adjunct to their daily routine. It is their routine. Therefore they become masters of discipline. They learn to zig as long as they have to. But they still face the same problems as the sometime creator. They use the subconscious to work over the creative problem. They organize. And they are usually prepared for right-side activity when they sit down because they've made the transition from left to right. Because their livelihood depends on how well the right side works, they, like firemen, are ready for the call. That's why, often in the strangest places, you'll see them jot something down on a note pad or the back of an envelope, get a glazed look, and sooner than later leave to start working. The simmering pot has boiled over and some ideas have reached the conscious. It's why creative professionals are often late or undependable or suddenly nonappearing when they're expected at social occasions. And it's one of the things their partners or husbands or wives have to understand and learn to live with.

In one area the person who has a creative avocation has an advantage over the professional. The amateur or semi-pro is deeply interested in what she's doing. The professional often is not. I don't mean that we all don't heave long sighs when we have to tackle a publicity piece for a meeting of the local garden club or the fund-raising approach for the volunteer ambulance corps. That's paying your dues for being known as creative. ("Suzanne can do it. She writes such funny letters.") I'm talking about doing what you like to do. I've seen it in the eyes and enthusiasm of friends who are working in watercolors or are taking night courses in short-story writing or directing the Little Theatre group. They can't stop talking about it. And they can't wait to get at it. With these people, how long they zig at one time is usually not a problem. The greatest danger they may face is working too long, going beyond the right side's capacity as it gets tired. Frustration sneaks in. And then, perhaps obstinacy, culminating in discouragement.

> **LEFT SIDE:** C'mon kid. It's getting late. Let's call it quits.

> **RIGHT SIDE:** Quiet. I think I'm getting it.

> **LEFT SIDE:** That's what you said an hour ago and I don't notice anything happening.

> **RIGHT SIDE:** I know it'll work out here. If I could only get this characterization right, everything will fall into place. But something isn't working and I don't know what it is.

> **LEFT SIDE:** You're so tired you wouldn't know it if it stood up and flashed you.

> **RIGHT SIDE:** That's about the kind of wit I'd expect from you.

> **LEFT SIDE:** That's because I'm not creative. C'mon, let's pull down the shades, kiddo.

> **RIGHT SIDE:** No. I'm gonna keep at this until I get it.

> **LEFT SIDE:** Suit yourself. But don't call on me because I plan to be elsewhere.

> **RIGHT SIDE:** (muttering) Maybe I never should have started this thing. Maybe I'm just not good enough. Maybe I should throw the whole thing out . . .

> **LEFT SIDE:** Maybe you should put everything on the back burner and slip into the arms of Morpheus. It'll look better in the morning.

And so it will. And right side's interest should be rekindled with a good night's sleep so that the next time, which in this case should be as soon as possible so that the frustration doesn't build up a block, the right side can reach into the pot refreshed and come up with some ideas.

part four

PUT IT DOWN: USING THE RIGHT SIDE TO GET IT ON PAPER

chapter 22

PSYCHODYNAMICS

Up until this point I've tried to keep these short bursts or tips on creativity as general as possible, but while I was gathering material and letting things percolate my right side kept nudging some ideas specifically for writers into the foreground. The left side resisted.

> **LEFT SIDE:** Hey! This book is for everyone. You start concentrating on writers and you'll lose all of the other people who are working at being creative in other fields.
>
> **RIGHT SIDE:** Yeah, but—
>
> **LEFT SIDE:** But nothing. Some businessman walks into a book store and picks up your book and hits this psychodynamics-and-the-writer-nonsense and it's no sale.
>
> **RIGHT SIDE:** Yeah, but—
>
> **LEFT SIDE:** I've beat my part of the brain to a pulp trying to organize this thing and keep you on strategy and now you wander off this way.
>
> **RIGHT SIDE:** Yeah, but—
>
> **LEFT SIDE:** (sighs once more) But what?
>
> **RIGHT SIDE:** —but I want to say something. I think it's important and—and—I think it'll help some people zig, maybe.
>
> **LEFT SIDE:** (beseechingly) Why? Why me?

And so the next few pages will have some zigging hints for writers. I do think, however, that anyone interested in

developing the right side will get something out of it. Try it
and see.

When writers develop characters for a piece of fiction, a
play, or script, they sometimes have a hard time deciding
exactly who the characters are, what they stand for, what
motivates them, how they develop or don't develop. We all
use experience and insights as a guide, but sometimes the
lines get blurred. That might be the time to explore psycho-
dynamics, which relates to the relative strengths of the personality traits of an individual—a kind of psychologically
oriented biography. In marketing it's often used to try to define and follow the inner workings of people's minds' which
may both respond to and in turn define certain life-styles.
Companies and advertising agencies use this kind of analy-
sis to guide them in appeals they use in positioning their
products and developing new products.

For example, the current intense interest in health and
the worship of physical fitness mark an obvious life-style
trend that influences both of these areas. Who ever thought
that rowing machines would be a multi-million-dollar indus-
try 15 years ago? Or that over 17,000 people would run,
romp, stride, wheel, and stagger through the five boroughs
of New York for 26 plus miles once a year? Or that hospi-
tals would receive a growing portion of their income
through preventive medicine programs? Psychodymanic research might help us not only to identify these trends but
also to discover what motivates them. And this kind of motivation could play an important role in an author's character development.

Clyde works out on Nautilus equipment two hours every
day. Why? Because it makes him feel better? Because he's
insecure? Because it compensates for his failure in other
areas? Because he's vain? Because he's nervous about his
looks and thinks bulging pectorals will make up for it? Because he's ambitious and wants to build up his resistance to
stress? Because he's scared of dieting?

This may seem as though we're working backward, and
perhaps we are—but that's another form of zigging. Most of

the time we try to use research to reach a conclusion. In this case we start with the conclusion (popularity of exercise) and try to find out how and why we got there. Think about it. You're trying to decide what kind of traits your hero should have so that you can develop his actions and dialogue with a certain consistency. You know that in your plot development he will be physically challenged at the climax. But you want this to come as something of a surprise to the reader. Also, for the plot's sake, he is a technician in the laboratory of a large metropolitan hospital.

Your character's development might go something like this. For reader credulity in the physically taxing climax scene, he must be in excellent shape. Make him an exercise nut. Body building and endurance. What kind of person exercises as a part of his regimen and why? (See above.) Now, if these are the traits of a Nautilus nut—insecure, vain, compensating for failure, shy, or ambitious—which ones would fit our hero? You decide that insecure and shy are exactly right and you begin to develop his actions, habits, mannerisms, and dialogue along those lines.

I think this method of zigging was nicely illustrated in the late 1970s movie, "Marathon Man," where an important element of the plot was the hero's addiction to running. He ran against the clock around New York City's Central Park reservoir. This activity, of course, plays an important part in the climactic scene when he is chased through the streets of the Lower East Side by gun-firing villains. They're great physical specimens. He is Dustin Hoffman. But he gets away because he can run forever—and they can't. The activity also helps develop the hero's character as a loner and a person of perseverance. Because running has become so much a part of the scene of our times, the plot twist and character personification did not seem forced.

In the advertising business we do psychological interviews to uncover these sometimes hidden characteristics and motivations, but by using logic and some common sense you can probably do your own simplified interviews among friends and cohorts. If you know of someone who has a particular habit or characteristic—fastidious, sloppy, avuncular, whatever—observe closely and try to figure out what other traits or habits that particular mannersim might lead to or explain. And using this zigging technique, working backward, you can figure out quite a bit yourself—even as I did with the case of Clyde, the Nautilus nut.

chapter 23

PEOPLE, PLACES, AND NAMES

Character names. Often bothersome, always important whether in a novel or short story, play, movie, soap opera, advertising campaign, or even lyrics for a song. The trouble is we often don't realize this and just pick any name because we're concentrating more on plot development or dialogue or a deadline. We don't really want to waste time on a name at that point and anyway a name is what you make it, right? Well, perhaps. But I think that many authors underestimate the power of names in building an image for the character. In a world of zigging, there is one area, however, where we might want to consider zagging along with the rest of the people. In some instances the obvious, the cliché names may help more with characterization. Mention Harry or Harvey in the world of television commercials, for example, and the klutz who lives next door or the bumbling husband comes to mind. Edna may be Harvey's wife. Wanda, the voluptuous but featherbrained cousin. Myrtle, the gossip who lives down the block. Craig and Joanna the lovers. What ever happened to Bob or Mike or Jim or Steve or Barbara or Betsy? When you have to create an image fast, as in the 30-second television commercial, it's often best to put these names back in the file and stick with the clichés. (You just wouldn't name the boob who chose the wrong power mower Pete or Johnny or Rod.)

Some years ago I was involved in an advertising campaign for Gold Medal Flour. The objective was to create brand awareness among younger flour users. We created a series of radio commercial interviews in which the first man

> To mention a loved object, a person, or a place to someone else is to invest that object with reality.
> —Anne Morrow Lindbergh, "Baker Lake," North to the Orient

to walk on the moon (this was four years before Armstrong and Aldrin took their giant steps for mankind!) announced that the dust on the moon's surface was actually Gold Medal Flour and that the springy step he took was not from the lack of gravity but rather because the moon was made of a Gold Medal sponge cake (the dark half was chocolate cake). It got attention.

We felt that one of the most important parts of the idea was the astronaut's name. We spent days working on this. Very important because the hero was to play a continuing role in succeeding commercials. We finally settled on Commander Brad "Skip" Wheelright. In my opinion it was a name that truly worked for us in creating the image we wanted—a believable yet tongue-in-cheek cliché. To this day I fully expect to read his name as commander of some space shuttle.

One of the problems with selecting names is that we often tend to be too neutral. "Oh," we say, "no one would ever have a name like that. It's too ludicrous." Ha. Then's the time to stop and think of some of the people you know. Unbelievable names are everywhere. Here are some from my experience: Harvey Waffle, family doctor; George Argetsinger, friend of my grandfather; Enis Agletinger, a secretary; Green Fenley, copywriter; Gray Beverly, account executive; Gabor Apor, producer; Ray Wray, acquaintance; Elihu J. Michenoff, B-24 navigator (no flying today because they called the Michenoff); Lieutenant Sunshine, pilot— who seldom smiled.

Again, the idea is to let the names work for you. The master of this, of course, was Charles Dickens. Fagin and Smeed and Scrooge and Nicholas Nickleby and Bob Cratchit. Marvelous. And so are the modern-day characters of Bob and Ray; Wally Balou; Mary Backstayge, noble wife; Dr. Mu, Hawaiian eye, ear, nose, and throat specialist. And the names are just as important in serious works.

One of the problems that many of us have is the tendency or almost uncontrollable desire to use real names because we've written a story based on real people. The names are a part of the association. You know it was the Hogan twins who used to get undressed nightly before an undrawn shade, offering an anatomical education to a group of quivering 12-year-olds. But the public doesn't know. To them the names might just as well be the Sweeney twins or the O'Brien twins. For legal reasons you should probably make this change. Once you do, as long as the names fit the characters, you'll begin to believe that their real name was Sweeney or O'Brien.

Place names should also work for you. Garson Keillor didn't name it Lake Crystal or Lake Sunrise. In my favorite radio show of the past, "Vic and Sade," people came from Dismal Seepage, Ohio, or Fishigan, Michigan (home of Rishigan Sishigan). But if you want them to sound authentic and not necessarily rib-tickling use authentic names and switch states. I don't mean New Orleans, Kansas, or Los Angeles, Pennsylvania, but rather make Ridgefield, Connecticut, Ridgefield, Wisconsin, a quiet town in the hills along Route 8. Or Port Townsend, Washington, a busy little port city in Pennsylvania on Lake Erie.

Many authors do use real locations, of course, and in minute detail. They take us down streets we know and into familiar buildings. It's fun, rivets our attention, and builds a feeling of realism. Frederick Forsyth is a master of this as his hero walks up London's Sloane Street and then left through Harrod's and out the great Food Hall to Knightsbridge. It gives a feeling of actually being there. And if you have been there, the scene becomes a familiar picture and backdrop for the fictitious characters who suddenly take on a new reality and increased believability.

Generalization is necessary to the advancement of knowledge; but particularity is indispensable to the creations of the imagination.
—Thomas Babington Macaulay,
"Milton"

chapter 24

DIALOGUE

Don't skip this section if you're one of the many who think that dialogue is the sole province of the novelist, playwright, or script writer. Or even the nonfiction writer (note that I've used it quite a bit in this book). I believe it's an underused art that can find a place in almost any form of communication. While the novelist moves the plot along or develops characters or creates a mood with dialogue, there are many places for it in the more usual forms of everyday communication. It can be used to illustrate an idea, emphasize a point, or set up a theory, among other things.

You are a member of the governing body of a small village. You are composing a letter to all of the homeowners in your village urging them to attend a meeting with a neighboring village to work out some common guidelines concerning condominium development in the area. Unfortunately, an earlier meeting had resulted in divergent points of view leading to accusations, recriminations, and bad feeling on both sides. You could start this way.

> I'm writing this to urge all of us to rethink our positions in regard to Bricktown's condominium development. We must try to consider all points of view (ours and theirs). For those of you who may have missed the last meeting, it turned into a name-calling contest. Not only was nothing decided or accomplished but etc., etc.

But how about putting a little zig in the approach?

The Scene: Bricktown Village Hall
The Time: 9:06 P.M. last Tuesday

A man is hid under his tongue.
—Ali ibn-abi-Talib, *Sentences* (7th century)

99

The Occasion: Joint Bricktown-Shad Run "What are we going to do about the condominiums" meeting. A voice is heard from the back of the room. "It seems to me that if the self-satisfied people of Shad Run would do a little more thinking about the good of the river front as a whole rather than their own precious little village we . . ."

"I resent that, just because . . ."

"And I resent your trying to tell us what to do . . ."

"People . . . people . . . please . . . order . . ."

"Oh you do, do you, well let me . . ."

And this meaningful dialogue went on for two hours and 43 minutes. It stopped at 10:30 because by then no one was speaking to anyone else. Bricktowners and Shad Runners were even bickering among themselves. Obviously, we can't continue this way if we're going to try to work out solutions to the problem. I suggest, therefore, etc., etc..

Perhaps the dialogue version is not as quick. But it is more dramatic and attention-getting and it illustrates the foolish impracticality of the tenor of the meeting—particularly for those who were not there.

You're a teacher and you must write the parents of an overly voluble student about some problems he's creating.

Dear Mr. and Mrs. Becker:

At the beginning of the fall term as an exercise in communications, I asked my second-grade class to tell me what they did in the summer. To start them out I told them what I had done when I was young. My family lived over a delicatessen and I spent one summer delivering for Mr. Cohen, the owner. In fact, on one Saturday I delivered, to a bar mitzvah, the largest order he had ever put together.

Me: "Class, it was 122 loaves of bread, seven quarts of dill pickles, 42 sliced onions, 33 pounds of cheese,

Speech is the mirror of action.
—Solon (7th–6th century B.C.) quoted in Diogenes Laertius, *Lives and Opinions of Eminent Philosophers* (3rd century A.D.)

and 155 pounds of sliced meat. I was so proud I rushed home to tell my family and do you know what my father said?"

Your son: (wiggling his eyebrows à la Groucho Marx) "That's a lot of baloney."

Of course the class roared and even I smiled. That was the second day of school. Unfortunately, it set the tone for your son, and over the past few weeks, the situation has continued to deteriorate so that I think it's time we met and etc., etc.,

Here the dialogue helps to ease the parents into the situation without the usual confrontational approach. In addition, it also helps to position the teacher as a person of humor, understanding, and warmth.

Obviously the best dialogue writers have an ear for speech patterns and can develop a rhythmic flow that can build suspense, excitement—any number of moods. Good dialogue can build a scene with no descriptive phrases. No news here, but it's an art to be practiced and developed. Too many writers think they have to adhere to the he said—she replied—he exclaimed school. Not so. Even at the turn of the century, authors were utilizing different approaches. Notice how Owen Johnson did it in one of his famous Dink Stover stories. The scene is a moonlight night on the Yale campus. Dink's friend, Tom Kelly, having spent a happy evening imbibing the grape, is now trying to hit the moon with pool balls. Another friend, Dopey McNab, tries to reason with him.

"I say, Tom, old fellow, you know me, don't you? You know I'm a good sort, don't you—one of the finest?"

"I know you, Dopey McNab, I'm proud to know you."

"I want a word with you seriously."

"What?"

"Seriously."

"Say on."

"Now, seriously, Tom, do you think you can hit it?"

"Don't know; going to try's much as in me. Biff!"

"Hold up," said McNab, staying his hand. "Tom, I'm going to appeal to you as man to man."

"Appeal."

"You understand—as man to man."

"Sure."

"You're a man; I'm a man."

"The finest."

"Now as man to man, I'm going to tell you the truth."

"The whole truth?"

"Solemn truth."

"Tell on."

"You can't hit it."

"Why not?"

"Tom, it's too—too far away!"

The two shook hands solemnly and impressively.

I was delighted to see, in a recent public television adaptation of a Lawrenceville piece, that a good bit of Johnson's dialogue was used verbatim—and it wears very well.

While many good writers come by this talent instinctively, there are some tips that can help anyone improve his or her dialogue skills.

1. Use a tape recorder to pick up casual talk around the living room, dining-room table, or at a party. But be sure you explain what you're doing and get permission from the participants. At first they'll be self-conscious, but only in the beginning. Then listen to it later, to the inflections, the colloquialisms and mannerisms, the phrases, the accents.

2. Outline a scene and see if you can create the images through dialogue alone. This was a device that radio writers of the 30s and 40s had to use but obviously it has fallen into disuse in the past 30 years. While you're doing this, don't cheat by putting descriptions in the mouths of your characters.

Don't do it this way: "C'mon out, Charley. I see you hiding in that 1982 Buick with the golden retriever in the back seat parked in front of Phil's Hardware."

But rather do it this way: "I think I see him.

"Where?"

"In the Buick in front of Phil's Hardware."

"What'll we do?"

"I dunno—I'll yell."

"Geez, I'm scared."

"Me too, but we can't let him get away."

"Hey—there's a damned dog in the back seat."

"Yeah. It's a golden retriever, though. They're friendly.

"I hope so."

"C'MON OUT, CHARLEY.

3. Always read dialogue aloud. See if it sounds the way you want it to sound. But remember, it may vary according to the medium. Dialogue to be read should be written to be read, while dialogue for TV or a movie or a play is written to be heard. Example.

Dialogue to be read:

"What the hell you talkin' about, Harry? You're off your gahdamned nut."

"Nah, I was just thinkin' about the broad. I mean, she's a slut but she's, you know, an okay slut. Except for the friggin' fur hat."

Same dialogue, written to be heard:

"The hell you talkin' about, Harry. Off your gahdamned nut or somethin'?"

"Naw. I was just thinkin' about—you know, thinkin' about the broad. I mean she's a slut but she's, what the hell, you know, an okay slut . . . except for the—for the friggin' fur hat."

The dialogue to be heard uses repetition, broken sentences and speech patterns that we are used to and that our ear and mind accept and automatically translate. But if this dialogue is for a novel or short story it becomes confusing and boring. One of the best writers of contemporary dialogue is Elmore Leonard. Look how he blends both of these modes so that when you read you can actually hear the speech. In fact, it's hard to read Leonard without at least whispering to yourself what's being said. Now that's dialogue writing.

. . . a writer should create living people; people not characters. A character is a caricature.
—Ernest Hemingway, *Death in the Afternoon*

". . . you have a cigarette?"

"I quit while I was in the hospital."

She said, "Yeah, why get cancer when you can get shot."

She said, "Donovan, the big shit, he tells me I can have my own band. I get here, I've got one number I do. 'Automatic,' the Pointer Sisters? These guys, they get on their roll I don't even know what they're playing. They're spazzed out on ganja anyway, they don't give a shit, they're gone. 'No Parking on the Dance Floor,' the Midnight Star number. I'm on the synthesizer? I'm tryin' to keep it precise, these guys ride right over you."

Words, phrases, references, asides all strung together to advance the story and at the same time to establish the character and the mood. Notice that you really don't have to understand all of the patois to know what's going on. It's so good that not one descriptive phrase or reference is needed.

4. Do a piece of dialogue of a certain period. But try not to use the present idiom. Research the language and idiosyncrasies of that period. It's a great way to bring the reader or listener into the world that you're talking about. And it reinforces authenticity. However, be careful of using language of the past that may make the story stilted or interfere with the flow. In a screenplay that I did which took place in the 30s I used phrases like "Hot spit" and "Put the kibosh on that idea" but not "Everything's hunky-dory" or "That's the bee's knees." The first two seemed to me to be natural and unobtrusive. The last two are forced and, I feel, would interrupt the thought process no matter where they appeared.

5. When you use dialogue to help define personalities, be consistent. Again, in the "Vic and Sade" radio show, Vic, the father, always greeted his son Rush with a different put-down name. "Whadya say, downspout" one day. "Why hello there, flyswatter" the next and "Where's your mother, curbstone?" The faithful radio listener recognized this warm semisarcastic imaginative approach as part of Vic's character and looked forward to these wayward appellations from show to show. And the writer, Paul Rhymer, seldom disappointed them.

Notice that often people who are somewhat insecure use the three-repeat habit. With many of them it becomes a speech pattern. Listen to people around you in crowds.

> "Know what I think?"
> "No, what?"
> "I don't think the Mets are gonna make it this year."
> "Yeah. I agree."
> "No sir. Not this year."
> "Yeah."

> **How strange are the tricks of memory, which, often hazy as a dream about the most important events of a man's life, religiously preserve the merest trifles.**
> —Sir Richard Burton, *Sind Revisited*

"The Mets are not gonna make it this year. That's what I think an' you can take it or leave it."

Not only do we have the thought repeated three times, but often even the same words. Be judicious in using this technique, however, because as you can see, it can slow down the story. But it can add believability and character development. You know who the people are.

6. Most of the time in writing we strive to avoid the cliché. In dialogue writing, according to the image you're building, the cliché can often be useful and a lot of fun. If you're developing a character who's talkative and boring, keep a list of clichés and worn-out-from-overuse sayings that can be selected lovingly when needed. An all-time record breaker happened to me the other day when a man informed me that a certain person was ". . . in over his head but fast out of the blocks so we'll watch him like a hawk." Three in one sentence! I won't mention such modern favorites as prioritize (or any other ize, for that matter) and parameters. By the time you read this they'll be old hat or will have sunk like a stone or (insert your favorite here.)

chapter 25

GIVE THEM MORE THAN THEY EXPECT

One of the most rewarding parts of the creative process is the extra something that's added to the main thrust of a creative project. In some of our most popular novels the author lets his characters comment on the passing scene, having nothing to do with the plot but a lot to do with an attitude—and the characterization. It's not necessary, but it's nice. John le Carré is a master of this. So was the late John D. MacDonald, who often philosophized on the foibles of mankind through the mind and eyes of Travis McGee.

Cole Porter and Johnny Mercer did it with unexpected rhyming and meter. They often put couplets together where they weren't needed. Notice this from Porter's "I Get a Kick Out of You."

> I get no kick from a plane
> Flying so high with some guy in the sky is my i-
> dea of nothing to do
> I get a kick out of you*

High, guy, sky, my, i (dea). He didn't have to do all that. But isn't it wonderful. Mercer also did it with his voice and that mellow, easygoing attack, sliding up to the note.

The author Joseph Kastner in his book *A World of Watchers* chronicles birdwatching, America's oldest sport. One of the things that make the book so enjoyable is the extra dimension he gives to the birders—and not just in relation to their avocation.

"He (Spencer Fullerton Baird) was apparently born with the urge to make lists. As a boy in Carlisle, Pennsylvania, he listed the money he got and spent, the books he lent and borrowed, the ages of the members of his family (he had not been able, he admitted with the scrupulousness that marked him later as a scientist, to obtain the ages of two aunts), and of 'songs that I sing' (although the family did not remember his singing, only whistling)."

Can't you just see him? The book is full of these delightful extras that make it and its inhabitants, feathered and otherwise, come alive.

These are sometimes subtle but always important ways of enhancing the creative approach that can perhaps intrigue and reward your audience. But the little ways count, too. Al Hirschfeld, the great caricaturist, has for some years included his daughter's name at least once in all of his drawings. Aficionados look for the number beside the artist's signature in the lower right-hand corner, indicating the number of hidden Ninas in that particular drawing. In our family we had Sunday-morning contests to see who was the quickest Nina finder.

I think one of the nicest things about these somewhat hidden little creative extras is that they reward you, the creator. It's nice if the reader or viewer or listener gets it but if he doesn't, so what. You liked it. The something extra. The creative secret that makes you feel good.

part five

UP AGAINST THE WALL

chapter 26

BEATING THE CREATIVE BLOCK

We've all heard about it and many of us have experienced it. The dreaded monster. The seemingly insurmountable wall that rises out of nowhere and keeps things from happening. It brings with it agony, trepidation, fear, frustration, anger, insecurity, and sometimes, if it can't be surmounted, defeat and failure. Fortunately, most professionals have learned to deal with it. For the others who use creativity as an adjunct to their lives, the mental block is not as devastating. But it is still something we don't relish. And if we don't learn to handle it, it can eventually lead to less and less creative thought, work, or experimentation because the block becomes self-perpetuating. We get ourselves in a spot where we don't want to start something because we're afraid we can't finish it so we taste defeat before we even begin.

One of the ways to keep the block from insinuating itself into your right side is to be sure you have a strategy or plan or set of objectives. If we know where we're going it's easier to get there. Or the corollary, when we don't know where we're going we have a tough time finding the way. This is the creative block hiding under the guise of lack of knowledge and/or planning. So, to stop it before it starts go back and read Section 11—Right-Brain Strategies.

If we use the left-side–right-side theory we may be able to shed some light on procrastination (an offshoot of the block) and how the anticreative left side might help. Remember, the right side is working in its mode, the left side

> **I don't want the cheese, I just want to get out of the trap.**
> —Latin American proverb

has subsided. Suddenly there's no activity from right side. And left side notices.

LEFT SIDE: Oh oh. What's going on? Nothin' comin'?

RIGHT SIDE: (confused) Yeah . . . I dunno . . . I mean I can't seem to be able to work this out.

LEFT SIDE: Well, what the hell, kiddo. Maybe you should bag it. Take a rest. Let's go downstairs and read the paper. Or see what's on TV. Or even have a drink. It's almost five o'clock anyway. Besides, if you want my opinion, I didn't think it was such a good idea to begin with.

RIGHT SIDE: No I don't want to read the paper or look at TV or have a drink and you never think any idea is a good idea until it's done. Why can't you help me, instead of sitting there telling me all the other things I could be doing?

LEFT SIDE: Help you? I am helping you by showing you there's more to life than this silly creating you seem to want to spend a good bit of our time doing. What else can I do?

Every exit is an entry somewhere else.
— Tom Stoppard, *Rosencrantz and Guildenstern Are Dead*

Lots else. Left side can be a big help by reminding right side of the aforementioned strategy or plan. And if this doesn't work, by suggesting other routes. First, by acting as a sounding board. As in most quandaries in life it often helps to talk the situation over with someone else. Whether or not she suggests a solution is not the key thing. (If she does, wonderful. But most of the time she doesn't.) The important point is you are able to formulate your own thoughts better by hearing them as you talk. So if there's no one to talk to, train your left side to be that back board. Do this by actually talking out loud and writing down your reasoning and thoughts. This is another way to clarify thinking and direction.

Of course, the type of project you're involved with also has much to do with how you may possibly overcome the block. Some people say, "Just start doing it." At least you're doing something and that sometimes can get you going. Yes—and no. In writing a report or composing a show tune or jingle or preparing an advertising campaign that can lead to big trouble—particularly if you're good because the execution may not be leading you anywhere. Again, because you have no plan or strategy. As I said before, a plan or specific strategy is one of the keys to creative stimulation. And stimulation is the key to a door in that wall that may be blocking us. Even the creative act of flower arranging can benefit by a plan. The Japanese tradition of Ikebana couples formula and reason with creative flair so that, while people with great right-side leanings can do wondrous things, even the left-siders can learn how to produce some surprisingly imaginative and interesting creations.

If, however, you're handling a less formalized creative project—a painting or even a script for a play or movie or a piece of poetry or lyrics for a song—it sometimes does help to just start doing it. At the same time, in a visual creative exercise like painting or photography I would first go through the exercise of looking at what the greats have done. Try to rekindle the inspirational fires. Then talk yourself into an attitude of experimentation. Don't think that what you're doing has to be the finished work for posterity. Try a grey, brooding sky and see what that does. And if it doesn't work out, try something else—a hazy, brassy, almost orange sky. Stay loose and pretty soon the right side will be back in the groove, nudging and suggesting and "what ifing." Zigging once more.

In writing a screenplay I've often started a scene with just a general idea of what I want my characters to do and then let it, or them, develop as the scene unfolds. If it seems to be going in a strange, unplanned direction I let it work along to see what's going to happen. Often it's the wrong direction. But within the dialogue or action there may be an interesting something that leads to another approach, and I can incorporate it in the next rewrite. And suddenly it comes together and there it is. The breakthrough—an unmatched joy. That to me is one of the great creative rewards.

chapter 27

WHEN ZIGGING DOESN'T MAKE IT

Failure.

That's what your project turns out to be. A failure. You worked so hard. And you had such high hopes. You thought it was a smashing idea. But somehow, some way it turned out not to be different, not to be brilliant. Oh, they were nice.

"Why, I think it's . . . it's very good, Ardis."

"Yes . . . how long did you work at it, Ardis?"

"Three weeks—on and off."

"That long? I mean—uh—that's a long time—ah—I admire you for your perseverance."

"Yes . . . it certainly is a tribute to your—ah—it certainly is something."

"Well thanks—but I'm not very happy with the way it came out, personally."

"Oh now, Ard, it's perfectly all right. It'll do just fine. After all, that's a pretty ambitious project you took on . . ."

"Yes, Ard . . . we love you anyway."

"Well, thank you very much and you can all go perform obscenities on yourselves."

And, of course, you determine never, never to get involved in a creative project again, even though you were having fun while you were doing it. Hold the phone, friend.

The only impeccable writers are those who never wrote.
—William Hazlitt, *Table Talk*

Failure is the constant companion that all people who dabble in any way in creativity learn to live with—or at least coexist with. And if you're discouraged over something that didn't make it, talk to someone else with an active right side. Mention the subject and he'll pour out a litany of failures that will make the sinking of the *Titanic* look like the pinnacle of success. Every zigger has them because you can't reach for something without missing occasionally. Or to put it another way, he who doesn't cross the street will never get hit by a car. But he'll never see what's on the other side, either.

So learn to accept the fact that if you're going to try to zig you may have to settle sometimes for even less than second best. But when you do make it, it's worth all of the failures put together.

A good example took place in the National Indoor Track and Field Championships recently. The great Russian world record holder in the pole vault, Sergei Bubka, decided to pass several lower heights and wait until the bar reached 18′ 9¼″. He had made that height several times and felt that he could start there and go on to the stars. The chance he was taking was all or nothing at all because if he missed, after having passed all of the previous heights, he would finish last because, obviously, he would have cleared no height. As I recall, the only person left to compete against him was Earl Bell, a veteran who had won his first championship 11 years before. Both missed on their first two attempts. Bell on his last vault seemed to float down the runway and rose to the heights almost in slow motion. His legs made it, his knees, his chest and then he flung his arms up and cleared it by half a foot. On his final vault, the champion took his time concentrating, pacing his steps. The crowd was suddenly silent. it was a poem in motion in the hush of the Garden. He seemed to lift off in two stages with an extra boost at the end that put him a foot higher than the bar. But he was too close and smashed it coming down. He was out. He took the big chance—and finished last. But what a sensation it would have been if he'd made it on the first vault. He walked up to Earl, his conqueror of the evening, and shook his hand. He knew what the risk was. He knew the taste of defeat. And everyone knew that he'd be back next week. Perhaps to take the risk, to do it differently, to zig again.

But if he's smart, he'll learn from his failure. He'll realize that perhaps he works better taking the earlier vaults. Obviously, his timing was off and that could have been because he waited too long. In any kind of disappointment or defeat, we should regroup and learn. But somehow it seems harder for creative people. Possibly because the right side is more sensitive. Laurel's answer to Hardy's criticism was to scratch his head and cry because the creative process seems so personal. No one else to blame. That's why I always preferred playing soccer to running on the track team. In soc- no one but you. Once as a college freshman I was ignominiously defeated by a high-school senior in a quickly arranged warm-up meet. Oh, the disgrace of it all. Searching for some kind of comfort I asked the coach what he felt went wrong. He thought for a minute and then turned to me and said, "The problem is—you didn't run fast enough."

Which brings up another point about failing. There is and will always be someone who can run a little faster. But that doesn't mean you should ever stop trying.

Experience is not what happens to you; it is what you do with what happens to you.
—Aldous Huxley, *Reader's Digest* (March 1956)

chapter 28

CRITICISM

There is criticism—and there is criticism. Most of us are used to the two kinds, personal and impersonal. The impersonal seems to come with projects, activities, or jobs that we've been working with or on, often with a number of people. Because the criticism seems to revolve about the result of what we were doing rather than how it was done or who did what, it's easier to accept calmly and coolly. Naturally, the fewer people involved in the project the more the criticism edges toward the personal, which is harder to take because it moves from the logical, less emotional left side to the very emotional right.

Large wounds in the ego can become a reality if the creative person isn't prepared for these facts of life. It's tough. And that's why we often don't ask for comments or criticism. You know you should have someone look objectively at what you've done and give you opinions, but everything inside rebels against this. And so the creative right side spends a lot of time slyly and deviously building up some ways to bend, deflect, or even stop any critical evaluation of its efforts. Here are some of those ways that the left side must be aware of and put a stop to.

1. Don't let right side make excuses. "Listen, I want to get some opinions, but it's not ready yet." Or, "I'm really not in the mood right now. Let's do it another time." Or, "I'm too busy with another project but I do want to do it, honestly. How about sometime next week?" Or next month. Or next year. The next thing you know left side will be saying "Well, this is another fine mess you've gotten us

> Literature is strewn with the wreckage of men who have minded beyond reason the opinion of others.
> —Virginia Woolf, *A Room of One's Own*

119

into. Now it's too late to do anything about them, even if we did get some comments." Which, of course, is exactly what right side has been angling for.

Every vice has its excuse ready.
—Publiluis Syrus, *Moral Sayings* (1st century B.C.)

People ask you for criticism, but they only want praise.
—Somerset Maugham, *Of Human Bondage*

2. Don't let the right side throw a temper tantrum at the first sound of "The problem I see here is. . . ." These kinds of outbursts may be a natural part of the right-side personality. Over the years, there have probably been attempts to keep it under control. But right side craftily sees that a temper can become effective in blunting criticism because most critics will just say it's not worth it and subside accordingly. And thus these outbursts become a calculated tool and weapon.

3. Sulking, pouting, and tears are other tried and true devices. They inhibit critical honesty perhaps not as dramatically as the tantrum but they lead to, "I didn't have the heart to really get into the big problem . . ." and some helpful comments go unvoiced and unrealized.

4. But perhaps the subtlest ploy of all is to nod, listen, even make Gee,-I'm-glad-you-said-that-I-never-thought-of-it-that-way statements—and then never do anything about it. This will work once, maybe twice. But eventually the critic will not want to criticize. Waste of time. I give it a lot of thought, and he nods—and doesn't pay attention. The offshoot of doing nothing, of course, is to make token corrections of a few of the little things but ignore the principal criticism under the guise of, "Look, I listened and did some of the things you suggested."

It's like changing your earrings and ignoring the large spot on the front of your sweater.

With those cautions in mind, here are some ways you can prepare yourself for the inevitable, and wanted, comments that will and should come.

1. While you've been creating you've presumably worked yourself into the right-side mode. Now, in the stage when you're looking for an appraisal of your work, right side must subside and left side must take over, rational, methodical, businesslike. One way to achieve this is to try to take yourself out of yourself when you ask someone for comments. Pretend that you're the messenger delivering the goods. "A friend of mine asked me to bring this to you and get your comments and then relay them back." It's kind of a "Gee, that's a good idea, I'll tell him when he comes in" role for the left side.

2. Don't let right side barge through to argue or defend. Explain to clarify, yes. But if too much explanation is needed, that in itself can be a warning signal. Perhaps the idea or thought or visual communication isn't coming through as clearly as you planned.

3. Don't be too eager to agree with everything that's said, either. Articulate critics can sometimes make everything seem logical. They've sold you. But when you get back and dissect their criticism, everything else falls apart. Now this may not be too important because, after all, you can just ignore the comments if you don't believe they're right unless the critic has some control over what happens to what you're doing—say, an editor, owner of an art gallery, or producer. In my business, this is a constant problem. You don't want to lose the idea by seeming stone-headed and obstinate. But by agreeing without some deep consideration and thought, you run the risk of at least changing the thrust or watering things down so that you've neatly entered the ordinary world of the zagger.

I, at one time, had proposed an advertising campaign built around a soap opera format. Each commercial was designed to make the viewer think that she had come upon a new soap opera. The product was deftly inserted in the middle of the commercial as an answer to the problem that the dramatic situation had set up. Then—and this is where I failed—I wanted to return to the main theme with a non sequitur that had nothing to do with the original drama, much as we see daily in the popular soaps. Example:

WOMAN: (breathlessly) What about Diana?

MAN: (seriously) The mortgage is assumable.

Or this one, I think my very favorite:

WOMAN: . . . but where's Frank?

MAN: He's incognito.

WOMAN: In where?

Now, remember. These quick endings had nothing to do with anything else. We presumed that the viewer would assume that Diana and Frank were people that had appeared in another episode, even as we do when we see promotions for the soaps. I'm not sure that the presumption was right but I felt that once the idea took hold we would have a popular and looked-forward-to bunch of commercials. Others were worried and they talked me into changing the endings to one-line gags.

WOMAN: I stand on my principles. Why don't you leave?

MAN: Those aren't principles you're standing on. It's my foot.

I gave in because I wanted to save the idea. But by changing the ending I had abandoned the satire of the soap opera approach. Anyway, it didn't work. That probably had little to do with the changed ending. But I'm not sure. And I would have felt better if I'd gone down with all flags flying.

4. If possible, know your critics' likes and dislikes and habits. I have one friend who comes on very strong, ranting and raving and ripping things apart. My left side squashes the rising right side and I sit back and let the critic go. And pretty soon he begins to put things back together again and mutter, "Actually, this part isn't so bad" and soon he gives me cogent comments that I've always found most helpful.

But if I didn't know him I would probably have stalked out of the room. Which suggests that we at least hear our critics out before any kind of rebuttal, if a rebuttal is needed.

5. There's a thin line between criticism and reaction. Reaction is usually an instant response given by anyone who's around. It tells you what people think and feel—but not what to do. Criticism should be given by someone you respect because criticism usually leads to suggestions.

6. In summary, the four steps in receiving criticism should be to listen, discuss (not argue or necessarily defend), think, and act.

chapter 29

STEP BACK. MAKE SURE YOU'RE NOT ZAGGING WHEN YOU THINK YOU'RE ZIGGING

. In the beginning of most creative efforts we work with theories that build into amorphous ideas. Some of this comes from hard concentration, some from the pot on the back burner, some from group interaction. Most ideas are stimulated by something. In fact most ideas are rearrangements of other ideas. Not that they aren't original, in their own way. They are, but make sure.

Sometimes the stimuli seem to be in the air around us, brought on, perhaps, by a series of events that seem unrelated. For example, our recent leaning to the past, to nostalgia, may be a result of uncertainties about the future. We're grasping for what we perceive as a simpler, more orderly life. This gives birth to a rock-and-roll revival for those who see the 50s as the simpler life. It may also be one of the reasons why we have a sudden rash of coming-of-age movies set 30 and 40 years ago. Neil Simon and Woody Allen mined this lode to good advantage with "Brighton Beach Memoirs" and "Radio Days."

The point is that when that idea comes and you leap up screaming "That's it," sit down immediately and get something rough down on paper. Then step back and make sure that that really is it. Make sure not only that it works but that it hasn't been worked before by another in the same

> **In good writing, words become one with things.**
> —Emerson, *Journals*

> **A writer is unfair to himself when he is unable to be hard on himself.**
> —Marianne Moore, interview, *Writers at Work: 2nd Series*

way. Now, if you discover that it has, that doesn't mean abandon ship. Just be aware of it. Change your idea so that you won't be walking in the same footsteps. And watch out for the temptation of saying, "It's somewhat similar, but mine is much better." Somehow it comes out like writing a *Gone with the Wind* clone, changing the name to *Burn Atlanta Burn* and the heroine to Tiffany Finnegan and claiming that it's different.

All of this is another reason to have an uninvolved person take a look at it before you proudly present it to your public. But don't feel bad if the great idea suddenly begins to look like someone else's or everyone else's. Go back and see if you can find what the stimulus for the idea was. Then, if you think it's valid, use that same impetus to accomplish what you want differently. See if it can get you zigging in another direction.

chapter 30

ZIGGING PRESSURE AND STRESS

Many people use creativity as an outlet to relieve pressure and stress that may come from another source. It can be particularly soothing in cases where there's a mood induced by a problem that's unsolvable. As a matter of fact the outside worry or problem can sometimes force the heavy right-sider into the kind of concentrated creative mode that we're constantly striving for. But the concern has to be so great that we seek refuge in another activity. I've known creative people in the advertising business who have done their best work when trying to escape from the cloud of tragedy.

The creative mode becomes a form of therapy, and while it can't make the person feel better instantly it does occupy the mind almost completely and relieve the gnawing, constant emotion—whether it be grief, sorrow, fear, or despondency—until time has its chance to begin the healing process. Keep this in mind the next time you're faced with something that you can do nothing about.

But be sure that there really is nothing that can be done about whatever is plaguing you. If there is, face the challenge. Do it. And don't bury your head in the creative sand.

What's more common, however, is the pressure and resultant stress brought about by the creative activity that we're involved in. And whether or not you're a pro, a semi-pro, or a dabbler in the stimulating world of the right-sider, the enemy is most often the one mentioned in the introduction—lack of time. Those that work for a living as copywriters, artists, playwrights, novelists, nonfiction writers, directors, architects, composers, arrangers, soloists, inventors,

> As every man is haunted by his own demon, vexed by his own disease, this checks all his activity.
> —Emerson, "Fate," *The Conduct of Life* (1860)

and just about any other occupation that you can think of that produces something that has to meet any kind of schedule are familiar with the crush, the sword that dangles over the head, the sands of time running out until that dreaded day when someone asks, "Where is it?"

As I write this, in the back of my mind is the phone call that I'm afraid to make to my editor saying that I don't think I'll finish on time. And I know that he has a printing schedule, sales meeting, and publishing date to meet in order to take advantage of the mass of orders that I'm sure will swamp him for Christmas giving. I worry about this. I have doubled up my writing schedule. I write on planes as I travel. I write every night and weekends. Will I make it? Somehow, I will. This comes from over 40 years of experience meeting deadlines. You learn how to adjust on the back nine. If you let the pressure get to you, you soon choose another profession.

This should not be true for the heavy left-sider who's trying to develop the sleeping right side for fun, psychic reward, or familial adulation. Actually, if this person is having scheduling or time problems, then he's not as strong a left-sider as one might think because the left side should take care of these things. Remember, the left side is the businesslike planner. "Watch it, kid, you're taking on too much. Don't promise that by the 30th, we'll never make it. I'll tell them to push it back to the 10th."

The problem is that in these pressure situations, it's the right side that takes the beating. Not by getting something done on time but rather by not ever getting started. Because those wonderful three hours on the weekend that you were going to spend on oils or needlepoint or practicing to play a clarinet in the style of Jimmy Noone disappear into the maw of time consumed doing something else. "Honestly, I've been trying for three weeks to get to my watercolors but I just don't have the time."

As I said earlier, I'm afraid the big problem is that we're living in a society that's becoming more and more the slave of time.

What can you do about it, other than quit, pull up stakes, and head for that South Sea island where creativity is making small coconuts from large ones? Well, I've found that a few things help.

1. Let the left side be the policeman. Plan. When things begin to mount up, sit down at the beginning of the week and make out a schedule. While we all need relaxation, you'll be surprised at the amount of time that you spend sitting around having the extra cup of coffee or talking on the phone or browsing through magazines. In the high-pressure world more time is spent in meetings that go on too long because they're not organized or perhaps not even needed. Or in writing memos that are two pages too long. Or having a lunch that goes on and on and accomplishes not much unless you consider another half inch on the waistline your noontime goal. With left side becoming a momentary time-motion engineer or pseudo efficiency expert, it is not unheard of to pick up an extra couple of hours a day. And those hours, used in creative activity, can take you away from your everyday world, transport you into new adventures where the contrast alone can help reduce pressure and stress.

2. Exercise! Trite. Overdone. The "in" thing. But it is terrific in holding down the blood pressure and weight, not to mention the occasional semi-euphoric feeling that some people claim. (Not me. I run and I find the best thing about it is taking a shower when I'm finished. But it does relieve my tensions and stress.)

3. If you do have some kind of deadline to meet, let your left side figure out how much time the job will take. And then when you start to do it, do the best you can in the allotted time. But use the time wisely. Don't keep straining and reaching for that big idea right up until the last minute. Because if it doesn't happen, the stress of fear of failure will mount. This may go against the previous advice of not

Killing time is the chief end of our society.
—Ugo Betti, *The Fugitive*

It seems no more than right that men should seize time by the forelock, for the rude old fellow, sooner or later, pulls all their hair out.
—George Dennison Prentice, *Prenticeana*

being afraid to fail. But, again, striving for the creative breakthrough takes time. And if you're on a very tight schedule, you have to plan your attack and efforts accordingly.

4. If you're not ready, if even the ordinary isn't coming, if what you're going to do looks as if it might be an embarrassment, try to recognize this more than 15 minutes before the deadline and do what I hope I don't have to do. Ask for more time.

Plans get you into things but you got to work your way out.
—**Will Rogers,** *The Autobiography of Will Rogers*

part six

SELLING IDEAS: THE ZIGGER'S WAY

chapter 31

PRESELLING YOUR AUDIENCE

While a creative accomplishment can be rewarding to the creator and fill the right side with delight and self-satisfaction, most of us want someone else to see, become involved in, and appreciate our work. We do not look askance at the "Why, Madeleine, I didn't know you could do that type of thing. It's wonderful" comments. Deep down and although we may not admit it, we work at our projects with a primary objective of being recognized for our talents. And, of course, the budding semipro or professional has a layer of people—editors, project directors, designers, publishers, or producers—between herself and the public that must be listened to and satisfied as the project goes forward.

> To hear great poets, there must be great audiences too.
> —Walt Whitman, "Ventures on an Old Theme," *Notes Left Over*

All of this points to another phase of creativity.

Selling the stuff.

Some pure right-siders might say, "Nonsense (or phooey or no way), a creative product must stand on its own. It's either successful or not. You don't have to be sold on Michelangelo or Browning to appreciate their works." I think that might be true if we were all pure right-siders with the capacity to automatically become a part of the wavelength that these geniuses are working on. Obviously, we're not. That's why courses are taught in Shakespeare and galleries give guided tours at a Matisse exhibition. They are explaining the creative thinking and reasoning and doing of the artist, with all of the contributory factors, so that we may understand, appreciate, and enjoy the work more and better. In doing this, they are selling because this kind of understanding promotes a larger audience.

But when, during the creative process, do you start selling? When it's finished, you say. Yes. But that may not be the only time. If it's something that you hope to sell, you usually start at the beginning idea stage. An outline for a book. A theme for a series of paintings for a gallery. A concept for a fund-raising letter. The left side becomes heavily involved in this selling process because it's the articulate side. It takes right side's thesis and explains it. After left side's job is done, and presuming that the selling is successful, right side swings into action and the mode of creative concentration takes over and sublimates left side's urge to constantly check and see how things are going or to show it to someone else as "work in progress," gawfabid.

Left side should listen to and respect right side's judgment. There are often reasons why this pre-exposure is important. But right side knows when the time is right. Too soon and you may rattle the confidence of the person to whom you're baring your work (the showee). Too late and you may have done a lot of work in vain that must now be corrected. On the other hand, some right-siders want to keep everything under wraps because if it's not shown to anyone, it can't be criticized. Another challenge for the balance between left and right.

Anyway, here are some guidelines that I've found helpful in preselling your audience.

A man without a smiling face must not open a shop.
   —Chinese proverb

1. Know who they are. If they're knowledgeable in your field the presell should be easier because they can probably visualize and know what you're talking about at any stage of development. If they don't have as much creative flair, you should know that and gear things accordingly. Don't leave too much to the imagination. If you don't know anything about the sellees, err on the side of conservatism.

2. Show and tell should become tell and show. Presell before you show them what you're doing. Never say, "I want you to look at something and then I'll explain it later." Later may be too late. Opinions have been formed. Walls may be starting to go up. And when criticism comes through lack of understanding, you have to start back-pedaling, which begins to build a defensive mood. And you're now pre-unselling.

Often the presell can be done well in advance of the showing. What we're trying to do is get the sellee in the right mind-set to accept what we're doing. If we've taken a remarkable zigging route, if what we've done is different from the norm or what we think he's expecting, then it's most important that he be prepared. It's been my experience that as soon as you're sure of your route you should start preparing the sellee. Of course, you may not be sure. Right side may be reaching and experimenting. More presell. "Gary, one of the things I've always admired about you is your willingness to try different things. We're doing something like that right now and I know you'll understand when I say we should take this chance and see etc."

3. In many cases preselling must include a form of educating the sellee. If you're developing a fund-raising drive for the Pee-Wee Hockey League and you're basing it on increasing costs you must educate the sellee on the increased price of hockey sticks, pucks, rink rental, and other daily ice-time items. If you're developing a screenplay and you want to give the sellee a feel for the locale, you might want to use location slides. Sometimes, to evoke a location or mood, we use scrap—pictures cut from magazines or other publications that illustrate a certain feeling we might be striving for.

In certain situations the consumer's beliefs or perceptions, discussed at some length earlier, can be a big help in setting up the climate for the presell. If you're involved in creating a strategy to prevent developers from building on a meadowland along a river bank, you might start by presell-

Understanding is the beginning of approving.
—André Gide, Journals

ing the governing body that controls such things on the value of wetlands for the continued existence of certain forms of fish, plants, and wildlife. This goes against the preconception of wetlands as useless swamps. You could use examples of how, in similar situations, the quality of life was reduced. All of this is designed to help presell the sellee on a point of view or frame of mind so that when the actual presentation of the material is made it has a better chance of being fairly received and perceived.

4. If you can control things, try to do the preselling in the form that's best and at the time that's best appreciated by the sellee. Of course this presupposes that you know something about the sellee's habits, likes, moods, and dislikes. This kind of intelligence can be invaluable. Try to come by it. It could prevent such gaffes as trying to presell someone by inviting her for cocktails and finding out, too late, that she's a Mormon. You'd make a point—but it would probably be the wrong one. Again a case of unsell.

5. Plan your presell carefully. Know exactly what and how much you wish to accomplish. Try not to get carried away and spill the beans. Here's what I've seen happen.

Late one afternoon, a creative director has just finished a long treatise on why it's most important to do something different to get attention in advertising today. He's been most dramatic and persuasive, illustrating the different moods of the television viewer over the years, which have gone from intrigue and interest to insult and ennui. The sellee (client in this case) has been most attentive. And then the mistake.

> **CREATIVE DIRECTOR:** Well, I'm glad you see my point, Earl, because that's why it's important to do something to break that boredom barrier that exists today.
>
> **CLIENT:** Couldn't agree more, Jack.
>
> **CREATIVE DIRECTOR:** Glad you agree because what we have for the new beer campaign is certainly different.

CLIENT: Oh . . . like what?

CREATIVE DIRECTOR: Well . . . I wasn't going to get into this, but what the hell. It's so unique. Essentially what we're going to do, Earl. What we're going to do is . . .

CLIENT: Yeah, yeah.

CREATIVE DIRECTOR: We're going to . . . get this . . . we're going to do the entire commercial without ever showing the beer—or mentioning the name.

CLIENT: (silence)

As you can guess, there was trouble in River City. The creative director made the classic mistake of getting carried away, after an excellent job of preselling, and going into the regular presentation of the material without having the material. The let-me-give-you-a-quick-preview approach seldom works when you're dealing with a zigging proposition because anything that's different needs more than a verbal description. (Actually, the idea was a good one. Using a musical theme that over the years had become the property of this particular brand quickly identified the product.) The presentation of the material itself must be as carefully thought out and planned as the presell was. Which is what we'll get into next.

chapter 32

THE ONE-ON-ONE SELL

As we said in the previous section, when you've finished doing what you're doing, it has to be presented to someone. Because your audience can vary from one to 200 or more, the techniques of presentation can vary accordingly. With that in mind, I've covered this topic in two sections. The first will deal with presentations to one or two people, the second with group presentations. In each there are some basic guidelines that everyone should be aware of. Remember, the idea that sits in the bottom drawer really isn't going very far. Someone's got to get it out, get it ready, and get it moving.

1. Determine to do something about what you've done. Again, to create something for the satisfaction of the right side is fine but it's so much better if someone else appreciates it as well. And try not to procrastinate because one of the world's great sinking feelings is to have a project all nicely outlined in the mind and then have it appear in front of the public. Your idea from someone else's right side. Some years ago I took my family, five of us, down the Thames in a 32-foot single-screw launch, the M/V *Princess*. It was an adventure. I am not a water creature. For those of you who have never experienced it, England's greatest river between Oxford and Marlow consists of 20 locks with a little water in between. And each lock takes precision maneuvering to get through. I tried to accomplish this with much shouting and waving of arms. The highlight was entering the Iffley lock sideways, something never before seen by the

> Ours is the country where, in order to sell your product, you don't so much point out its merits as you first work like hell to sell yourself.
> —Louis Kronenberger, *Company Manners*

delighted bank-side picnickers. It's also impossible to carry the honey bucket from the head to the various shore-side sewage systems without slopping it down the leg. Oh, there were all kinds of things that went on. It was a memorable and, in hindsight, a wonderful six-day trip. And, at the time, an unusual trip for Americans—as far as we could see, we were the only ones on the river. So I thought it would be a natural for the *New York Times* Travel Section. I outlined it and roughed it out and determined to finish it one day. I never did. But someone else did. A similar story appeared in the *Times* Travel Section a few months ago. And it could have been mine.

2. Know what you want to accomplish. And perhaps all you want is for someone to tell you what to do with it. Fine. That's what you want to accomplish. But most of the time most of us have some kind of idea as to what we want done. We'd like the poem published in a small esoteric monthly or the play produced by an experimental Little Theater group. We'd like to get agreement to present the case for a historic preservation at a town meeting, with the backing of the village council. Most of the time it's good to tell the sellee what you'd like before you start. Some of the time, and this usually takes some knowledge of the sellee, you'd like him to discover and suggest the next step himself. The old "I'd-like-your-advice" request.

3. Know your subject. Not hard if you've wrapped your right side around it for some time. But what if you're presenting a group project—your idea with contributions from others? You should know the reasoning behind all of the parts as well as though you'd done it yourself. In advertising, this is the big reason why we always try to have the creators present at presentations of creative material. They have the feel for it. They can answer questions that others may not even know existed. But if, for some reason, you can't be present when this important step is being taken, be sure that you spend time briefing whoever is going to do it in your place. And if there's no one to be present, get the

A moment's insight is sometimes worth a life's experience.
—Oliver Wendell Holmes, Sr., "Iris, Her Book," *The Professor at the Breakfast Table*

One who understands much displays a greater simplicity of character than one who understands little.
—Alexander Chase, *Perspectives*

right side involved in a covering introduction. But be careful that you don't oversell or make it so compelling and intriguing that it detracts from what you're selling.

4. Know to whom you're selling. We covered this in the presell section. Often we're not familiar with the sellees. They're names on a masthead or stationery or in a directory. Inquire around. Do some research. Find out everything you can about their likes, dislikes, mannerisms, and habits. It can't hurt. One of the people to whom I present ideas is a notorious interrupter with the out-of-left-field question, the kind that can completely fluster the presenter. It took me some time to realize that this was his way of taking charge. Once he had made his point he would settle down and say, "What's a matter, kid, you nervous? Don't be nervous. Wanna get ahead in this game, gotta stick to your guns. Now just settle down an' tell me what you want to tell me." Knowing this, I would always leave an opening for a question and then go into a kind of controlled fluster until he achieved, in his own mind, control. Then we went on. Those that fought him either lost or got nowhere— which is tantamount to losing.

5. Take the sellee into your mind. One of the ways I've found successful in making a creative point is to involve the sellee in your thinking. Step by step lead her through your reasoning until the opportunity comes for her to arrive at the conclusion herself. And when she does this she's become a part of your right side, a part of the creative process, and it's hard for her not to buy what you're presenting.

6. The presentation length and details should be directly related to what you're selling. If it's a long, involved piece, you should be setting it up but not giving it away. If it's something like a painting or piece of photography, you might be talking about a short paragraph describing what you are trying to accomplish or, probably even more important to a gallery owner, how your work can lead to additional examples built around the same theme or using the same technique or graphic approach. If it's a script or movie you should probably talk about the setting, the perceived conflict, the suspense, and the characters. In a script that I recently completed concerning growing up in the 30s in upstate New York, I did all of this and included it in the opening scene to set the tone of the thing and give an idea of the humor, dialogue, and interaction of the characters.

7. If you're doing a selling piece to raise money for investment in a project—say a new restaurant—then the selling piece itself becomes the creative pièce de résistance and obviously it takes all of the attention to detail and length that are needed to present the real creative challenge, the restaurant. Usually these pieces need no introduction. They must stand on their own. But the guidelines described here certainly apply to the in-person presentation of the piece.

8. Listen, listen, listen. After you've made your introductory remarks and the sellee has had time to digest your work, listen to his comments. All the way through. Don't spring to the defense right away. Hear the sellee out. Here's where left side has to take over once more and control the emotion. Keep cool. Try to be objective. Remember, the comments and critique may actually be helpful in gaining the final acceptance of what you're doing.

9. When you leave the meeting be prepared for the second thoughts. I've seldom heard anyone say, "I like it. Let's go," first time around. It's usually "I like it, but . . ." or "I like it. I'll get back to you." The I'll-get-back-to-you approach can lead to "I've had second thoughts and . . ." And the "and" usually leads to some criticism. I don't think I've ever heard anyone say, "I've had second thoughts and I think it's wonderful." So be prepared for these later comments, too. Weigh them, rebut them, explain them, act on them—but be prepared for them.

10. Know when to give and when to hold the line. This is the toughest problem the right side has to face— even tougher than surmounting the creative blocks or getting into the creative mode because it pits emotion against

He who findeth fault meaneth to buy.
—Thomas Fuller, M.D.,
Gnomologia

judgment, creativity against practicality, ideas against reason, right against left side. And either side can be right or wrong or partly each.

Usually, in my experience, I've been able to anticipate what some of the major objections will be and at least have answers for them. When something comes up that I haven't anticipated, I step back and try to work it into the concept. Then I look again to see if the concept is changed or jeopardized. This is where it gets tough. Right side doesn't want any change. Left wants to do anything to get the thing sold. Somewhere in between there must be Solomon making a judgment. Put both the original and revised versions aside. Do something else for a day. Then come back and look again. Most of the time the answer is clear. If there's no difference, then lean toward the revise because you'll be throwing a bone to the critic who presumably has something to say about the final disposition of your work. They like that.

chapter 33

THE GROUP SELL

How many times have you been asked to say a few words to the folks here about such and such an idea? Or been told that you have to turn the research findings into a simplified slide show for presentation at the next meeting of the historical society. Or that, because you're her closest friend, you've been asked to be the key speaker at a testimonial dinner for the retiring family court judge. Or been told to present a synopsis of your allegorial drama to a group of 50 potential backers.

All of these involve both creative and presentation skills on a larger scale than you may be used to. And they should make use of different techniques than what you're doing for the one-on-one. Here are some tips for the group sell.

1. Again, know your audience. A little tougher than in the one-on-one situation, but it could be just as important. I say could be because obviously the likes and dislikes of the cultural society listening to a talk on historical houses are not as important as the makeup of the zoning board of appeals when you're trying to urge them to hold the line against condominium developers. You want to know who the key players are. Who the leaders and the followers are. Who the influentials are. Not that you neglect the others, but you want to make sure you're concentrating on the right person or people.

Once when I was a callow youth in the advertising agency business we had taken a group of clients on an annual outing to the Princeton-Cornell football game. I was a young copywriter and it was my first experience with client

The voice is a second face.
—Gerard Bauer, *Carnets inédits*

contact. I was determined to be charming and impress both the clients and my boss. We were to have lunch in a private dining room at the now defunct Princeton Inn. I was nervous. As we entered from the chartered bus, my boss hissed, "You're not mixing enough. Pick out one client and talk with him." I nodded and headed nervously to the men's room. When I returned to the dining room, people were chatting amiably in small groups, except for one rather distinguished looking gentleman in a dark suit who was standing somewhat alone surveying the scene. I zeroed in.

> **ME:** Great day for the game.
>
> **CLIENT:** Yes.
>
> **ME:** I think it's going to be a good one.
>
> **CLIENT:** Yes.
>
> **ME:** Nice trip down here.
>
> **CLIENT:** Except getting off the turnpike. That exit's tricky to find.
>
> **ME:** Ah—yes, but the traffic wasn't too bad.
>
> **CLIENT:** Not if you stay in the left lane.

It continued like this through lunch. I worked hard at drawing him out but the only thing that seemed to get any reaction was the trip from New York to Princeton. Finally we started for Palmer Stadium. Determined to move on to a more positive conquest, I left him somewhat smilingly contented and was immediately plucked by the sleeve by the boss.

> **BOSS:** What the hell are you doing? I told you to be charming to the clients.
>
> **ME:** I was. I was working on that client with the distinguished mustache but all he was interested in was the bus trip down here. Who was he, anyway?
>
> **BOSS:** The bus driver.

2. Once you know whom you're talking to, start planning on what you're going to say. And don't stop zigging. It's strange how some very creative people forget that they're creative when it comes to setting up and selling what they've spent a good bit of time, effort, and imagination doing. They may be great right-siders, but suddenly, when they're finished with their job, they retreat and let the left side take over. Perhaps it's momentary burnout. It's like being asked to run the relay right after you've finished a 3:58 mile. Got no more, kid. You work it out.

Lots of people cover this unconscious tactic with the ploy that the presentation is no place in which to be clever. "We should do it like everyone else does. Follow the formula. Do what's expected."

Resist this temptation.

Take a break after you've finished your project. Then come back, look at it again and put yourself in the creative mode to start planning on how you're going to reveal it. Work on the unusual. Consider slides, charts, scrap, videotapes (now extremely feasible with the camcorder). You'll be surprised at how effective visual aids can be. You're chairman of a committee to beautify your town or neighborhood. You're holding a meeting for volunteers. As in most of America, the first thing that's needed is an awareness of how slovenly we've all become. You walk down the street videotaping the three Norway spruces with the beer cans at the base, the old stone wall with styrofoam coffee cups caught in the ivy, the dented wheel cover, the discarded high chair, cigarette butts—the dreck of our lives sprinkled across everything that was once your town's pride. It's so commonplace that people treat it as a part of the scene—until your videotape wakes them up.

Use audiotape to record the reactions of some people to an issue. Very impressive—especially when they can't be at the presentation. "Mr. Chairman, I want to impress on you that I'm not alone in this concern. Listen to what some of your neighbors say about the need for a teen activities center . . ."

One who speaks aright never says his say at an unsuitable place or time, nor before one of immature faculties or without excellence. This is why his words are not spoken in vain.
—*Panchatantra* (c. 5th century), tr. Frank Edgerton

And while you're planning your persuasion be guided by one word. Empathy. How would I feel if I were on the receiving end? It's amazing how this putting yourself in the other person's seat can bring back a certain objectivity as well as some nice zigging.

3. Know when and where you're going to make the presentation. What's the shape of the room? Does it have electric outlets? Is the light adequate? Can it be darkened if needed? Can you be seen? Will you have to present standing up or sitting down? Is there a stand or podium or someplace to hold your speech or notes? If it's an evening meeting with a number of presentations, when will your turn be? Or will it be in the morning? Or right after lunch, when the troops tend to be little groggy? All of these questions lead to answers that can influence your planning and attitude. Don't overlook any of them.

Recently I was giving an illustrated report to a 40-man board of trustees. I had rehearsed it carefully—in my office. To keep it moving, I would pop the slides on behind me while I was breezing along. It took impeccable timing but it was as smooth as a just Zambonied hockey rink. Then we went to the meeting—a long hall with the projector at one end and the screen and me at the other. Instead of the usual extension cord and "pickle" for changing slides, this setup used an infrared beam that operated the slides just by pointing the small hand-held box at the camera. Fine. Until the 40 people entered and sat down—and blocked the line of the beam. Disaster. The smoothness that I'd counted on disappeared. Slides kept appearing late or not at all. Confusion. I finally had to finish the thing standing on a chair pointing the damned beam over their heads. Not the greatest way to make a somewhat serious, persuasive presentation.

4. Know what equipment you need and what's available. When in doubt, bring your own. Or make arrangements to have it there. "No problem," they say. "We'll have a videotape playback ready." Only when you get there, they have one that handles ½″ tape and you've brought ¾″. Or your slide tray doesn't fit their projector. Or no one can find an extension cord. Some people, if they're making a number of presentations, put together a simple emergency kit—small flashlights, masking and transparent tape, extension cords, plug adapters, black slides, pliers, screwdriver. These were lifesavers when we made about 15 different presentations in as many different rooms to sell the Take a Bite Out of Crime idea.

5. Now, I've made a big point of urging you to use your zigging abilities when creating the presentation. But be careful. Don't make the presentation or setup so exciting, so stimulating that it overpowers what you're trying to sell. We've all seen it happen in the movies. Imaginative opening credits that get you in an anticipatory mood—and it's downhill from then on. The theory is that what you're selling should be the climax, not an aftermax, of your efforts.

> A fool uttereth all his mind.
> —Bible, Proverbs 29:11.

6. Rehearse. Know your subject and make sure that your helpers know it as well. If you're presenting someone else's efforts, make sure that you know everything you possibly can about the work. Sometimes it's a good idea in these rehearsal sessions to present to a mock sellee, a friend who will give you uninvolved reactions. From what we hear, President Reagan regularly does this in preparing for his news conference.

If you're presenting in a situation where the sellee is providing help—a projectionist, someone to handle the lights, a chart holder—make sure that you brief her as well so that she knows the cues. It's important to make her feel a part of your team at the very beginning because you want her on board all the way.

7. Be prepared to change and improvise. Most of the changes that come about are because of time. "I know we said you have an hour, and I'm very sorry but Kate has to catch a plane and only has 35 minutes." Best way to handle this is to be prepared beforehand. Often we do a long and short version of our presentations. At the least, know

> The absurd man is he who never changes.
> —Auguste Barthélémy, *Ma Justification.*

what can be cut and telescoped if time becomes a factor. And if you see that the time thing is going to jeopardize your sale, do everything you can to reschedule the meeting so that you'll have enough time to do it justice. On the other hand, don't be so involved in the stuff that if they suggest cutting three minutes of your carefully crafted opening, you scream for justice and a new hearing. Let the left side step in and guide you.

8. There are other times when you should ask for a new or possibly a second presentation. If the key players are suddenly not available, proceed so as not to insult the underlings, but reschedule it for the decision makers. This also gives you a chance to rehearse the approach. If there is some outside force or event that takes place and diverts minds, if not eyes, reschedule at a time when you can have a better chance at full attention. Never make a presentation while the building across the street is burning down.

9. If you can control it, don't serve cocktails or wine before the presentation. For the obvious reasons, I don't ever like to make an after-dinner speech when I want to get some serious points across. Stuffed stomachs, wine, cocktails, and cigar smoke lead to droopy eyes and minds.

10. To read or not to read. If you're good at it you can get away with it—probably. But be sure that you're working from a podium or stand that's high enough to hide your papers and keep you from constantly dropping your eyes and talking into your chest. If you do read, practice scanning ahead, which allows you to look up halfway through each sentence. And if you tend to ad-lib, keep a pencil handy to mark your place so that there won't be a long stage wait and frantic searching when you return to the script.

Some people like to work from small cue cards and others from an outline. Of course, the best way is to know your subject and be articulate enough to do it without notes or script. The problem here is usually time. Few of us are disciplined enough to do this without wandering, which runs the danger of eating up time and watering down the impact. I like to make a presentation as much as possible from my head—but following an outline.

Don't read to a small audience, if you can avoid it. You may look both foolish and ill-prepared. You should really know what you're talking about well enough to be somewhat at ease in a small group.

11. If you haven't spent much time in front of a group don't worry about being nervous. Everyone is. As a matter of fact, I've noticed that when I'm not nervous, it usually turns out to be a performance less to my liking than when the shirt begins to get clammy and the palms slippery. A trick I've used is to pause and take several deep breaths just before going on. I like to think of it as pumping clear pure oxygen into my right side. The shakes calm down. Things get bright and crystal clear and everything seems to slow down around me. I enter a relaxed state and feel in command.

12. A few tips on what to do when you're on. Use eye contact. Pick out a few people in the audience and talk to them, obviously making sure that the decision makers are included. And I mean talk to them. Isolate them. Look them in the eye. But not for a long period. Switch to another but favor the decision makers three to one. And when you reach the climax and are asking for a decision, make sure you're not staring at the bus driver. Turn to those that matter.

If you have a microphone, don't worry about leaning into it. It's designed to pick up your voice. Just remember that if you leave the podium to demonstrate something while you're talking you're also leaving the mike and can no longer talk with that quiet confidentiality that is sometimes so effective when electronically magnified. Don't reach the climax, and say, "Let me show you while I explain the secret [step away from mike]. Now, as the blerfuss gabble grogle in your hand murleagle strum frenjhafer kronk [return to mike]. Now you know the secret. Isn't that something?"

If you are using a cordless lavalier mike, there's usually nothing to worry about once it's attached to you. A hand mike is good, too, as long as you remember to use it. And don't get tangled in the cord trailing along behind. These things do give you the opportunity to occasionally whip the cord behind you like a seasoned night-club performer.

Are your hands a problem? Don't know what to do with them? Use them to hold on to the podium. Keeps them occupied and can be a calming, steadying influence. But if you can, learn to use them. They can be marvelous assets in making a point, registering emotion, giving direction, beseeching, calming, exacting, stimulating. Ever see a cheerleader work up an audience without using her hands? Watch Johnny Carson or the master of them all on some of his old shows, Jack Benny. Practice in front of a mirror or on videotape and experiment with your hands. You don't have to use sweeping gestures, either. A flick of the wrist here, a deftly pointed finger there. They become moving accents.

13. Develop a very brief outline of the presentation. Of course, this may vary with what you're presenting. Before you start developing what you're going to say, go back to the five-point strategy. Ask yourself the guiding questions— what are the perceptions about what I'm going to present, whom am I talking to, what do I want them to do, what am I going to say to get them to do it, and what are the reasons that they should believe what I have to say?

Then break your presentation into a simple outline: background, buildup, the idea or project itself, summary, and, when appropriate, a request for action or a decision.

chapter 34

GROUP CRITICISM

Any kind of criticism is a problem for the right side because the concentrated mode that we've been talking about throughout this book tends to form a possessive cocoon around the work. I know some people who keep fiddling with their work, purportedly smoothing it out, when, in fact, they're stalling so that it doesn't have to be shown to anyone and thus cannot be criticized. One-on-one comments can be difficult but group criticism is obviously more difficult. Aside from the internal politics that may exist within any pecking order, we have the dominant personality challenge. This is where a persuasive member of the sellee group gets a groundswell going and influences all of the other comments. Fine if they're positive, but devastating if they're not.

One of the more difficult situations is where you are presenting your efforts to a group of people and must handle their questions and comments alone. Again, listen. Don't rush in to give a countering answer (a) before they're finished or (b) without thinking. Sound and obvious advice, but the right side often tends in this direction because it feels that any even slightly negative suggestions or comments are aimed directly at the creative heart and are designed to maim. Deep-breath time once more. Stay cool and give the left side time to get things in order.

If you have answers give them thoughtfully and clearly. Try not to vamp because it seldom works. If you don't have an answer admit it (not that you're wrong but just that you don't have an answer) and tell them you'll get back with further thoughts. Sometimes you may be representing a

> **There should be a dash of the amateur in criticism. For the amateur is a man of enthusiasm who has not settled down and is not habit-bound.**
> —Brooks Atkinson, "July 8," *Once Around the Sun*

153

team of people with your idea. Even though you may be the presenter, try to have some of them with you. They should be as conversant with what you're selling as you are because then they can play an important role in what I referred to in *The Creative Mystique* as the "selling ballet"—a verbal dance between at least three people. It works like this.

You finish presenting the material with something of a flourish. Your cohort quickly picks up and perhaps gives a few laudatory words of summary, carefully not overdoing it or repeating what you've already said (and never, never saying ". . . what Barbara's trying to say is . . .") and then asks for the next step—a decision, an opinion, a plan of action, whatever it may be.

This gives you time to catch your breath, think, and wait for the reply. The sellee asks a question. You consider it and answer. The sellee asks another question. Your cohort, who has been listening during your answer, fields this one. You listen and add on to her answer. Sellee comes back. Cohort's turn to answer. Back to sellee, to you, to sellee, to cohort, and so forth. The ballet has started from A to B to C to B to A to B. While one of you is in conversation the other has time to think, to regroup, to anticipate. As you can see, this can be handled with any number of people beyond three. But they must all be familiar with the project. And they must be cool, calm, and patient. Beware of the cohort who keeps interrupting or quickly jumping in with an answer. That will be the end of the graceful seller's ballet.

> A good critic is the sorcerer who makes some hidden spring gush forth unexpectedly under our feet.
> —François Mauriac, "A Critique of Criticism," *Second Thoughts*

chapter 35

WHEN YOU'RE THE CRITIC

We're always honored when someone says, "I wonder if you'd take a look at some work I've done and give me your honest opinions." But it can also open the door to some awesome responsibilities. I once asked a good friend, who happened to be an editor, to give me his thoughts on a piece I'd done. He liked it. "I'm glad," I said. He replied, "*You're* glad? I don't know what I'd have said if I didn't like it."

And there is the problem. How to be honest, helpful—and still maintain a friendship. Be aware of this when a good friend asks. If it's a really close friend your understanding of each other may surmount painful but honest criticism. But if the relationship is not so close you had better say something like, "I'll be glad to look it over but my opinions might not agree with yours. But remember, they're just my opinions. You're the one that's created this and you have a feeling for it. And after you've heard what I and others have to say, you do what your instincts tell you to do." This gets both of you somewhat off the hook.

Criticizing what the creator sees as zigging and you may see as zagging requires a combination of creative acuity, perception, and tact. It's again a situation where the left side and the right side should work together. Before you start, let the left side wipe the right side clean of any preconceptions about the person, the presentation, the subject matter, past experiences. You can't say any of the following to yourself:

> **A new idea is delicate. It can be killed by a sneer or a yawn; it can be stabbed to death by a quip and worried to death by a frown on the right man's brow.**
> —Charles Brower, Chairman BBDO, *Advertising Age*

> **The critic, to interpret his artist, even to understand his artist, must be able to get into the mind of his artist; he must feel and comprehend the vast pressure of the creative passion.**
> —H. L. Mencken, *Prejudices: First Series*

"I wish this guy would stop clearing his sinuses while he talks."

"Why did she do it in longhand? And for God's sake, why does she dot her i's with little hearts?"

"Oh boy, a piece on personal hygiene in state prisons among the elderly. What did I do to deserve this?"

"Another batch of cartoons. I wonder if they're as bad as the last which had captions with the sophistication of *Housewares Monthly*."

> **The first job of a critic is to be understood.**
> —Timothy Foote, author, editor, critic

When you're asked to give judgment you become a jury and you should try to be as impartial as a jury. One of the hardest things, for me anyway, is to separate the work from the person. Obviously it's much easier to be a critic for someone you don't know. But you still have to work yourself into the mode of the viewer or reader or listener—not the editor or graphic designer or composer. The stuff you're looking at may not be done the way you would do it but that's not the point. You must react as an audience and then become the critic.

Next comes the moment or moments of truth for you and the creator. The time when you sit down and tell him what you think. Some people write their opinions, which in a way is gentler because it forces them to develop the kind of tact that may slip by when they're doing it verbally. Here are some cogent points to keep in mind when you assume the critic's role.

> **Over the piano was printed a notice: Please do not shoot the pianist. He is doing his best.**
> —Oscar Wilde, *Impressions of America*

1. Be empathetic. Think of how you would like someone to criticize your work. And keep this feeling throughout the entire time you're criticizing.

2. Start with something positive. Anything. But make it as positive as possible. "Boy, you have a great style." "The subject you've chosen is just right." "I admire your subtle wit." "I can see you've put a lot of long hours in on this." "I don't know how you do this." The late Clifford Fitzgerald, the chairman emeritus of Dancer Fitzgerald Sample, used to always start with something like "I can't get over how you creative people think. It's marvelous and amazing the way your minds and imaginations work . . ." No matter what he said after that, we were basking in the glow of his admiration for our abilities. The positive start registers very high on the tactmeter.

3. If, in general, you like the overall project, begin with the accolade. This makes the specific criticisms easier to take. But if you're having problems with the concept, start with the details that you like and then segue into the big problem. Again, you've got them at least started in the right frame of mind. This positive approach also keeps them from becoming defensive and arguing every point, which negates the whole purpose of the exercise.

4. In your search for kindness, don't skip over honesty. In fact, try not to shade it. The person has asked for your opinion. If you agree to give it, then give it. Who knows, you may be right. And your creator may listen and do something about it. On the other hand, as we all know, honesty is not always the best policy. A few years ago when *The Creative Mystique* was first published, I was driving to New York with my 88-year-old mother in the back seat. She decided to read the book as we hummed along on I-91. I listened expectantly for the chuckles and mumbles of appreciation. Nothing. I looked in the rear-view mirror. She was engrossed. Finally, I could stand it no longer.

> "How you like it, Ibby?"
>
> "Hm. Oh . . . well, I think it's good—on the whole."
>
> "Whadya mean, 'on the whole'?"
>
> "Well, you know, in general, it's good."
>
> "Mom, that seems to indicate that there's something you don't like."
>
> "No . . . no . . . but you don't want me to just sit back here and say wonderful, sparkling, witty, insight—"

> **People can be induced to swallow anything, provided it is sufficiently seasoned with praise.**
> —Molière, *The Miser*

157

"Exactly. Those are the words I'm looking for. Keep going."

"But that wouldn't be honest."

And she went back to reading and I sulked the rest of the trip. When we arrived and had unpacked she brought the book to me and said: "I really do like it, Jack, but you haven't autographed it for me." And so I did, as follows:

"To Ib. Who over the years has been a great mother . . . on the whole. Love, Jack."

Honesty doesn't always have expected rewards.

5. Don't try to solve the problems as you see them. Just state them. If she asks for suggestions, that's different. But be careful of coming up with something off the top of your head. Be thoughtful—and know what you're going to say. A lot of this has to do with the relationship between you and the creator. If she respects you, you have to be very cautious with your comments or suggestions. She may act on them immediately because in her eyes you can do no wrong. And you may just have.

6. Many times good ideas are presented in too rough a form. Not enough work has been put into their development. Use this as a key to your criticism and urge the creator to spend more time on it.

7. One way to ease the sting is to use examples of other people, the more famous the better, who've had the same problems and have had to go back and work some more to overcome them.

8. Make sure that everyone knows what you're talking about—exactly what your criticisms are. This is particularly important if you're going to see the next revision. You don't want to be in the position of having to state your case all over again because they thought you didn't really have any comments.

> **I have never found, in a long experience of politics, that criticism is ever inhibited by ignorance.**
> —Harold Macmillan, *Wall Street Journal*

9. No matter what you've said before, at the end tell him how you admire the time and effort he's put into the project. And explain that while your criticisms are personal you offer them because he asked—and now you'd really like to see whatever it is he's done turn out great.

chapter 36

PRESENTATION DO'S AND DON'TS

1. Do be alert. You don't want to get things off to a smashing start by being heavy-lidded and foul-breathed as you limply shake hands with the sellee. This means watch your activities of the night before. Don't celebrate the completion of your work just before the presentation despite the temptation to say, "It's done! It's done! I don't care what happens tomorrow, I'm going to drink to finishing it tonight." This is particularly tempting when you're making the presentation away from home. There's something about a hotel room and a different environment that has a special lure. Resist it. Save your debauchery until after you make your presentation.

2. Do keep away from cigarettes, cigars, or pipes during the presentation, even if you think a meerschaum adds to your creative aura, unless you know the smoking habits of the sellee. And don't think that the "Do you mind if I smoke?" question will take care of it. There's a good chance that she will say no because she's being polite. But deep down she resents you for intimidating her and herself for not speaking her true feelings. Remember, as in any selling situation, you want to have as much going for you as possible.

3. Do review, at least in your mind, what you're going to say about a half hour before the meeting, even if it's a big presentation and you've spent the night before rehearsing. The quick scan of my notes puts me at ease and moves me away from the nervous how-am-I-going-to-start state

> Intemperance is the physician's provider.
> —Publilius Syrus, *Moral Sayings* (1st century B.C.)

> Mend your speech a little, Lest you may mar your fortunes.
> —Shakespeare, *King Lear*

into a cool, clear mode. With me it's like the zone the athletes talk about when everything seems to slow down and move gracefully into place. (Now, if I could only make this happen in tennis.)

4. Don't build challenges into your presentation. This probably will not be a problem for most of you, but it can become a subconscious habit for those who have to make a number of presentations—or if you have to make the same presentation a number of times. When we were developing the McGruff "Take a Bite Out of Crime" campaign I had to make the basic presentation to 10 or 12 different groups. It became somewhat tedious—at least for me. So I found myself building in challenges to make it interesting. What if I forgot the picture of McGruff? Could I do a good job with a detailed description? What if I forgot one of the scripts? Could I ad-lib it effectively? They were challenges, all right, but they were also minefields that could have blown several holes in the presentation. If this becomes a problem, go over the presentation and see how you can reword it or even restructure it with the idea of improving it—and at the same time eliminating the built-in boredom.

5. Do give credit to your cohorts if what you're presenting is a group effort whether your helpers are in the presentation or not. If they're there, they'll beam in appreciation. If they're not, they'll hear about it and be your faithful followers for life—or at least until the first time you don't give them credit. Remember, ego stroking is one of the greatest creative rewards.

In every work / a reward added makes the pleasure twice as great.
—Euripides, Rhesus (c. 455–441 B.C.), tr. Richmond Lattimore

6. Do know when to stop. And that's when you've made the sale or when you can do no more. And if you've made the sale, if they've said, "Wonderful. Let's go ahead with it," move quickly into the next step—which may even be, "Thank you so much. I'll be in touch with you shortly about the next step"—and then move out. Don't rehash your presentation or your project. The sellee has reached the apogee of interest. Don't help him start a downslide.

7. If you reach that point where you've done all you can and the sellee is not sold, then pack up the marbles and head on down the long trail of life, vowing to return another day with a new approach or project. Doggedly continuing to try to sell beyond the point of no return can do irreparable damage to any possible return engagement.

8. Don't try to respond to comments with a quick fix on the spot. Every now and then this works. But more often than not it doesn't and can lead to insecurity on the part of the sellee. When the sellee says, "I like it a lot but I have a concern over the motivation for the sex-starved hunchback," be wary of saying, "No problem. We'll change him to a harelipped federal judge who collects railroad ties for a hobby." Do say, "Hmmm. That's an interesting comment. I think I have an answer, but I'd like to go home and think about it. I'll get back to you quickly—but you do like it, in general?"

"Oh, very much. It's damned good."

What's happened is that by agreeing with his comment or at least offering to consider it and give him alternatives, you have brushed his ego, made him feel that he's contributed to the project and possibly made the project better. Remember, criticism is not automatically bad.

> Too much talk will include errors.
> — *Burmese Proverbs*

> The stones that critics hurl with harsh intent / a man may use to build his monument.
> —Arthur Guiterman, *A Poet's Proverbs*

chapter 37

WHAT DO YOU DO WHEN YOU'RE THROUGH?

Say "Wow. That's it." Or "Hot dawg. I've done it." Or "Whew!"

Pat yourself on the back because no matter what others say or do about what you've done, you're the one who did it. You have experienced the emotions of creation, of building something from your own right side, of accomplishing something that's yours—no one else's. You have suffered, groaned, struggled, rejoiced, sweated, and celebrated your way down the path to zigdom.

But be prepared for something else that will vary in proportion to the intensity of the effort you've put into the project.

The big letdown.

It seems to come with the arrival of the first free moment that was formerly dedicated to creativity. You find yourself wandering around aimlessly, lost, depressed. Of course, there's a cure. It's to continue prodding your right side into other creative endeavors, but not necessarily in the same field. Even the most swirling, dancing, energetic, inquisitive right side can get tired of working the same side of the street again and again without strolling through the park for a bit. If you've finished a watercolor of the Newfane, Vermont, court house in the spring, start to work on your rose garden. If you've polished off a long reminiscence about the rock scene in the 60s, get out the guitar and try some new chord progressions. If you've finally put together

> He that writes to himself writes to an eternal public.
> —Emerson, *Essays: First Series*

> When you finish a creative project, something that has consumed you for some time, it's like the end of a love affair.
> —Dr. Suzanne Eichhorn, psychologist

a complicated slide show, with pithy comments, for the historical society, enroll in a course in creative writing.

The object of this book has been to stimulate the creative abilities that we all have. If it has, don't stop now. Keep zigging so that you find yourself saying, "There's so much more that I want to do."

And then start doing it.